英語で楽しむ昔話

内桶 真二 編訳

はじめに

　本書は、一通り英語の勉強を終えた学習者が、英語で書かれた昔話を楽しく読みながら西洋文化の背景に触れ、またそうしながら自分を見つめ直す、そういった機会を提供することを目指しています。

　はじめから８つ目の話までは、見開きページで一話。本文のほかに、日本語訳、難しい箇所の注釈、そしてすべての単語の意味を載せています。日本語訳については、英語の理解を助けるような訳を心がけています。注釈を付けた箇所は難しいところです。英語らしい表現の箇所などもあります。最初のうちは、わからなくてもよいでしょう。やさしく書き換えることはあえてしませんでした。

　ここまでの話には、巻末に十分な練習問題を用意しました。練習問題は左側のページが読んだ話についての質問、右側のページが知って役立つさまざまなミニ知識という内容になっています。大哲学者の引用から、身近なキャラクターまで、固いものから柔らかいものまで、いろいろ取り揃えました。楽しみながら答えを考えてください。

　以上８つの話を何度も何度も、暗記してしまうほど読んでください。やがて読者の皆さんの血となり、肉となります。幼い子どもたちに読み聞かせをしたり、紙芝居をしたりする時にも、きっと一味違ったものになることは間違いありません。最初の８つの話のうち、気に入ったものを選んで、紙芝居を作ってみるのもよいでしょう。その際には話を書き換える必要があるでしょう。「キツネとカラス」の話に付いている練習問題が参考になることと思います。

最初の８つの話を十分に読み込めば、かなりの力が付いてくるはずです。本書は、ここまではたいへん親切ですが、９つ目の話から徐々に親切さが減っていきます。最後の３話では、「三匹の子豚」と「ブレーメンの音楽隊」には練習問題が付いていますが、「シンデレラ」には、練習問題はありません。また、はじめの８話では、すべての単語が載せられていますが、最後の３話では、原則としてその単語が初めて出てきたページにだけ単語の意味を載せています。さらに、「三匹の子豚」と「ブレーメンの音楽隊」には注釈がありますが、「シンデレラ」にはありません。つまり、「シンデレラ」まで読み進めれば（ここまで読み進めれば、自分がこれまで知っていた話とはだいぶ違っていることに驚くかもしれません）、日本語訳さえ手元にあればなんとか読みこなすことができる力が身に付いているはずです。ちなみに、外国語の勉強には対訳が一番だ、というのはサマセット・モームの見解です。

　授業でお使いいただく際には、はじめのうちは１話あたり、２時間から３時間かけて、ゆっくりと進めていくのがよいようです。特に最初は、練習問題の答えが出るまでに、かなりの時間を要することもあるようです。

　１人でも多くの方が、読む楽しみを存分に満喫してくださることを祈りつつ。

2006年２月14日

　　　　　　　　　　　　　　　　　　　　　　内　桶　真　二

Contents

はじめに	i
The Dog and the Shadow 欲張りな犬	2
The Wolf in Sheep's Clothing 羊の皮をかぶったオオカミ	4
The Farmer and His Sons 農夫とむすこたち	6
The Hare and the Tortoise ウサギとカメ	8
The Fox and the Crow キツネとカラス	10
The Fox and the Stork キツネとコウノトリ	12
The North Wind and the Sun 北風と太陽	14
The Goose that Laid the Golden Eggs 金の卵を生むガチョウ	16
Three Little Pigs 三匹の子豚	18
The Bremen Town-Musicians ブレーメンの音楽隊	28
Cinderella; or the Little Glass Slipper シンデレラ、あるいは小さなガラスの靴	44
練習問題	71

The stories are taken from the following:
    Aesop's Fables: A New Translation, by V. S. Vernon Jones. 1912.
    Cinderella; or, The Little Glass Slipper and other Stories, n.d.
    Household Tales by brothers Grimm, translated by Margaret Hunt, 1884.
    English Fairy Tales, by Joseph Jacobs, 1890.

英語で楽しむ昔話

The Dog and the Shadow

A Dog was crossing a plank bridge over a stream with a piece of meat in his mouth, when he happened to see his own reflection in the water. He thought it was another dog with a piece of meat twice as big; so he let go his own, and flew at the other dog to get the larger piece.

But, of course, all that happened was that he got neither; for one was only a shadow, and the other was carried away by the current.

欲張りな犬

犬が口に肉をくわえて、小川の上にかかっている木の厚い板でできた橋を渡っていると、偶然に水に映った自分の姿を目にしました。その犬は、別な犬が２倍の大きさの肉をくわえている、と思いました。そうしてその犬は口にくわえていた肉を放り出すと、より大きな肉を手に入れるために、もう１匹の犬に飛びかかりました。

でももちろん、どうなったかというと、その犬はどちらの肉も手に入れることはできませんでした。なぜなら、一方はただ水に映った影に過ぎず、もう一方は川の流れに流されてどこかへいってしまったからでした。

****

let go his own (meat) と肉を補って。letはlet-let-let。
all (← that（関係代名詞） happened) 起こったことのすべては

Q1 なぜ「別な犬」のくわえていた肉は倍の大きさに見えたのでしょう。
Q2 英語版のタイトルと日本語版のタイトルでは、どちらがよりふさわしいでしょうか。
Q3 この話から、私たちは何を学ぶべきなのでしょうか。
Q4 この犬のくわえていた肉はどんな形のものだったのでしょう？

all	あらゆること	meat	肉
another	別の	mouth	口
at	〜に向かって	neither	どちらも〜ない
away	去って、遠くへ	of course	もちろん
bridge	橋	only	〜に過ぎない
but	しかし、だが	other	他の、別の
by	〜によって	over	〜の上に
carry away	運び去る	own	自分の、自身の
the other was carried away もう1つは運び去られた 過去受動		piece	1切れ
		plank	厚い板
cross	渡る	reflection	反射、反映
was crossing 過去進行 渡っていた		see	見る
		shadow	影
current	流れ、波	so	だから、〜なので
dog	犬	stream	小川
flew	<fly at 〜に飛びかかる	thought	<think 考える、思う
for	〜なので	twice as big	2倍の大きさで
got	<get 手に入れる	was	<be、過去単数
happen	起こる	water	水
happen to	たまたま〜する	when	するとその時
larger	より大きい	with 〜 in his mouth 〜を口にくわえて	
let go	離す		

> 何度も何度も読み返しましょう。はじめのうちは単語の意味を確認したり、日本語訳を参照する必要があるかもしれませんが、やがて必ず英語だけを読んで理解できる時がやってきます。
> 　書き込みをするのも自由です。気が付いたこと、大切なことをどんどん書き加えて自分だけのホンを作りましょう。でも、ちょっとだけアドバイスを。いわゆる本文（英語のところ）には書き込みをしないようにしておくとよいです。その理由は、やがてわかるでしょう。

The Wolf in Sheep's Clothing

A Wolf resolved to disguise himself in order that he might prey upon a flock of sheep without fear of detection. So he clothed himself in a sheepskin, and slipped among the sheep when they were out at pasture. He completely deceived the shepherd, and when the flock was penned for the night he was shut in with the rest.

But that very night as it happened, the shepherd, requiring a supply of mutton for the table, laid hands on the Wolf in mistake for a Sheep, and killed him with his knife on the spot.

羊の皮をかぶったオオカミ

あるオオカミが、見つかる心配をしないで羊の群れを食い物にしようと、変装することにしました。そこで彼は羊の皮をかぶり、羊が放牧場に出てきた時に羊の中に紛れ込みました。羊飼いを完全にあざむき、群れが夜に囲いに入れられる時には、他の羊とともにオオカミも囲いに入れられました。

しかしたまたままさにその夜、羊飼いは食卓に羊の肉が欲しくなり、羊と思ってオオカミに手をかけ、即座にナイフで殺してしまいました。

****

resolved to disguise himself 変装する決心をした
in order that ～するために、できるように
he might prey upon ～を食い物にする
when the flock was penned for the night
　　　　一夜を安全に過ごさせるために、群れが囲いの中に押し込まれた時
requiring a supply of mutton = as he required a supply of mutton
　　　　彼は羊の肉の供給を必要としたので

　Q　あなたは日ごろ、どんなカワをかぶっていますか。
　　　また、それは何のためですか？

among	〜の中に	on the spot	その場で、即座に
as	〜のように	out	外に出て、放牧中で
as it happened	たまたま、あいにく	pasture	牧草地、放牧場
clothe oneself	〜の衣装を着る	pen	囲いに入れる
completely	完全に、まったく	prey upon	〜を襲って食う
deceive	だます、あざむく	require	〜を必要とする
detection	見破られること	resolve	決める、決心する
disguise oneself	変装する	rest	他のもの、残り
fear	おそれ	sheep	羊
flock	群れ	sheepskin	羊の皮
for the night	一晩	shepherd	羊飼い
for the table	食用に	shut in	閉じ込める、囲い込む
happen	起こる、生じる	slip among	〜に滑り込む
in order that	〜するために	so	だから、そして
in mistake for	〜と間違えて	spot	場所、点
kill	殺す	supply	食料、供給
knife	ナイフ	table	食卓、食事
laid	<lay hand on 手をかける	that very night	まさにその夜
might	<may できる	were	<be 過去、複数
mistake	間違い	when	〜の時
mutton	マトン、羊肉	with	〜で；〜といっしょに
night	夜	without	〜なしで
		wolf	オオカミ

---

skin cream（スキンクリーム）でskin care（肌のお手入れ）を怠らないのは結構ですが、そればかりに気を取られて、skin-deep（うわべだけ）な人間にならないように注意しましょう（ハイハイ、大きなお世話）。skin diving（スキンダイビング）で体と皮膚を鍛えるのもグッド。もしskin disease（皮膚病）で悩まされるようならdermatologist（皮膚科医）に診てもらいましょう。

ちなみに、こどもの発達に欠かせない「スキンシップ」は日本でつくられたことば、造語。濃い関係の、kinship（親族関係）、kin（親族、血族）＋ship（関係）をなぞったもの。英語では、personal contact や physical contactなどといいます。

Skinner（スキナー）博士はお好き？ skin+(n)er で「皮をはぐ人、皮はぎ」ではなく、行動主義の心理学者。

skin-headはちょっとキケンかも！

The Farmer and His Sons

A Farmer, being at death's door, and desiring to impart to his Sons a secret of much moment, called them round him and said, "My sons, I am shortly about to die; I would have you know, therefore, that in my vineyard there lies a hidden treasure. Dig, and you will find it."

As soon as their father was dead, the Sons took spade and fork and turned up the soil of the vineyard over and over again, in their search for the treasure which they supposed to lie buried there. They found none, however: but the vines, after so thorough a digging, produced a crop such as had never before been seen.

農夫とむすこたち

とある農夫が死の床に臨み、とても大切な秘訣をむすこたちに伝えようと願って、自分の回りにむすこたちを集めて言いました。「おらがむすこらよ、わしぁまもなく死ぬじゃろうて。だからのう、お前たちに知っておいてほしいんじゃわ。わしのブドウ畑にゃなあ、秘密の宝物が埋まっておるのじゃ。掘れ、そうすれば見つかるじゃろうて」

父親が死ぬとすぐ、むすこたちはスキやクワを手に取り、そこに埋められていると彼らが考えた宝物を探し求めて、何度も何度も繰り返しブドウ畑の土を掘り返しました。しかし、宝物は見つかりませんでした。でも、ブドウの木は、とてもよく土を掘り返されたあとだったので、それまでには見たこともないほど豊かな収穫をもたらしました。

****

being at death's door and desiring = as he was at death's door and desired
I am shortly about to die すぐに死ぬ定めにある
I would have you know お前たちに知らせるということをしたい
in their search for the treasure (←which they supposed to lie buried there)
　　　　　宝物 (←そこに埋められてあると彼らが考えた宝物) を探して
such as had never before been seen
　　　決して以前には見られたことがなかったような …

after	〜のあと	lie	ある、置かれている
again	また、再び	moment	重要性、大切なこと
am	<be、現在1人称単数	never	決して〜ない
as soon as	〜するとすぐに	none	ひとつも〜ない
at death's door	死を間近にして	of much moment	とても大切なこと
be about to	〜することになっている	over and over again	何度も何度も
been	<be、過去分詞	produce	生み出す、実をつける
before	以前、前には	round	〜の回りに
being	<be、現在分詞	said	<say 言う
buried	埋められて <bury	search for	〜を探すこと
but	しかし	secret	秘密、秘けつ
call	呼び寄せる	seen	<see 見る 過去分詞
crop	作物、収穫物	shortly	まもなく、すぐに
dead	死んで	so	そのように、とても
death	死	soil	土、土地
desire	〜を願う、望む	son	むすこ
die	死ぬ	spade	鋤（スキ）
dig	掘る	such as	〜のような
digging	掘ること	suppose	〜と思う、仮定する
door	ドア、入り口	that	〜と
farmer	農夫、お百姓さん	therefore	したがって
father	父、父親	there lies	ある
find	見つける	thorough	完全な、しっかりとした
fork	またぐわ	took	<take 手に取る
found	<find 過去	treasure	宝物、財宝
had	<have、過去完了を作る	turn up	ひっくり返す、掘り返す
have	（人に）〜させる	vine	ブドウ（の木）
hidden	隠された <hide	vineyard	ブドウ畑
however	しかしながら、それでも	was	<be、過去単数
impart	伝える、分け与える	which	関係代名詞
know	知る	will	（そうすれば）〜する
		would	〜したい

命令文 + and　〜しなさい、そうすれば...　　（聖書より）
Ask and it will be given to you; seek and you will find; knock and the door will be opened to you.
　　求めなさい。そうすれば、与えられる。探しなさい。そうすれば、
　　見つかる。門をたたきなさい。そうすれば、開かれる。(マタイ 7:7)

The Hare and the Tortoise

A Hare was one day making fun of a Tortoise for being so slow upon his feet. "Wait a bit," said the Tortoise; "I'll run a race with you, and I'll wager that I win." "Oh, well," replied the Hare, who was much amused at the idea, "let's try and see"; and it was soon agreed that the fox should set a course for them, and be the judge. When the time came both started off together, but the Hare was soon so far ahead that he thought he might as well have a rest: so down he lay and fell fast asleep. Meanwhile the Tortoise kept plodding on, and in time reached the goal. At last the Hare woke up with a start, and dashed on at his fastest, but only to find that the Tortoise had already won the race.

Slow and steady wins the race.

ウサギとカメ

ウサギが、ある日、とても足が遅いと、カメをからかっていました。「ちょっと待ってよ」とカメが言いました。「きみと競走しよう。きっとぼくが勝つと思うよ」「ああ、いいじゃないの」ウサギは、その考えをとてもおもしろいと思って、答えました。「やってみようじゃないの」そしてその場で、キツネがふたりにコースを設定すること、そして審判になることが決められました。競走が始まる時間になると、ふたりはそろってスタートしました。ですが、すぐにウサギはずいぶんと先へ行ってしまい、休んでもだいじょうぶだな、と思いました。そしてウサギは横になり、ぐっすりと寝入ってしまいました。その間も、カメはトボトボと歩き続け、やがてゴールにたどり着きました。結局、ウサギは、はっと驚いて目を覚まし、全速力で走り続けましたが、カメが先にゴールインしているのを見つける結果となっただけでした。

ゆっくりと確実なのがレースに勝つ（急がば回れ）

****

for being so slow (=because the tortoise was so slow) とても遅いという理由で
replied the Hare, who was much amused ウサギは返事した。そしてそのウサギはとてもおもしろがっていた
I'll wager that ～に賭ける、～だと思う
it was soon agreed that ～とすぐに意見が一致した
only to find that ～とわかっただけだった

agreed	<agree 同意する	meanwhile	その間に
ahead	先に、先方に	might as well	〜するのももっともだ
already	すでに、もう	much	とても
asleep	眠っている	off	start off 出発する
at	at last ついに、結局	one day	ある日
be amused at	〜をおもしろいと思う	only to find	〜と分かるだけだ
being	< be	plodding	<plod on とぼとぼ歩く
bit	a bit 少し、少々	race	競走
both	両者、ふたり	reached	<reach 着く、到着する
came	<come （時が）来る	replied	<reply 答える
course	（レースの）コース	rest	have a rest 休憩する
dashed	<dash 走る、急ぐ	run	run a race 競走する
far	遠く	said	<say
fast	fast asleep 熟睡して	see	try and see やってみよう
fastest	at his fastest 全速力で	set	設定する、設営する
feet	slow upon his feet 足が遅い	should	〜すべきである
		slow	遅い、ゆっくりとした
fell	<fall asleep 眠り込む	so	とても、だから
find	分かる、見つける	soon	すぐに
for	〜のために、〜の理由で	start	with a start はっとして
fox	キツネ	steady	一定していること
fun	make fun of 〜をからかう	thought	<think
goal	ゴール、決勝点	time	the time came 時が来た
had	<have 過去完了を作る	together	一緒に、ともに
hare	ウサギ	tortoise	カメ
idea	考え、アイディア	wager	賭ける、請け合う
in	in time 間に合って	wait	待つ
judge	審判	when	〜の時
kept	<keep 〜し続ける	who	関係代名詞
lay	<lie down 横になる	win	勝つ
let's	〜してみよう	woke	<wake up 目を覚ます
		won	<win 過去

Q あなたはウサギ派、あるいはカメ派、それとも何派？ 自分を動物にたとえてみましょう。ついでに、その動物になった自分の姿を絵に描いてみましょう。

The Fox and the Crow

A Crow was sitting on a branch of a tree with a piece of cheese in her beak when a Fox observed her and set his wits to work to discover some way of getting the cheese.

Coming and standing under the tree he looked up and said, "What a noble bird I see above me! Her beauty is without equal, the hue of her plumage exquisite. If only her voice is as sweet as her looks are fair, she ought without doubt to be Queen of the Birds."

The Crow was hugely flattered by this, and just to show the Fox that she could sing she gave a loud caw. Down came the cheese, of course, and the Fox, snatching it up, said, "You have a voice, madam, I see: what you want is wits."

キツネとカラス

カラスがチーズをくちばしにくわえて木の枝に止まっていると、キツネが彼女を目に止め、そのチーズを手に入れる方法を何か見つけようと、知恵を働かせ始めました。

その木の下まで来て立ち止まると、彼は見上げていいました。「上に見えるのは、なんて気品ある鳥だろう。彼女の美しさは比べるべきものもなく、羽毛の色合いといったらこの上ない。もしも外見の美しさと同じように声も甘くてすてきだったら、絶対間違いなく鳥の女王のはずだ」

これを耳にしたカラスは大得意になり、ちょっとキツネに歌えるところをみせようと、大声でひと鳴きしました。もちろん、チーズは下へと落っこちて、キツネはそれをさっと拾いながら言いました。「声はお持ちあわせのようですね、お嬢さん、それは分かります。足りないのは頭ですね」

****

coming and standing under the tree = when he came and stood under the tree
the crow was hugely flattered by this これによってカラスはとても得意にさせられて
and the Fox, snatching it up, said = and the Fox, after he snatched it up, said
what you want あなたに欠けているところのもの（足りない、ない、から、欲しくなるんですネ）

above	上に、上方に	observe	観察する、見て取る
are	<be 現在、複数	of course	もちろん
as ... as	〜と同じく...	ought to	〜のはずだ
beak	くちばし	piece	a pice of 〜の一切れ
beauty	美しさ、美	plumage	羽毛
bird	鳥	queen	女王
branch	枝	said	<say 言う
by	〜によって	see	見る、分かる
came	<come down 落ちる	set ... to work	〜を働かせる
caw	カラスの鳴き声、カー	show	示す、見せる
cheese	チーズ	sing	歌う
could	<can できる	sit on	〜に座る
crow	カラス	snatch up	拾い上げる
discover	見つける、発見する	some	何らかの
doubt	疑い	stand	立つ
equal	並ぶもの、同等のもの	sweet	甘い、すてきな
exquisite	この上ない、すばらしい	that	〜と
fair	美しい	tree	木
flatter	得意にさせる	under	〜の下に
fox	キツネ	voice	声
gave	<give （声を）出す	want	足りない、欠けている
get	手に入れる	was	<be 過去、単数
have	（声を）持っている	way	方法、やり方
hue	色合い	what	なんと（感嘆文を）
hugely	大いに、とても	what	〜の所のもの
if only	ただ〜でさえあれば	what you want	足りないもの
is	<be 現在、単数	when	〜の時
just	ただ、ほんの	with	〜を持って
look up	見上げる	without	〜なしで
looks	見かけ、顔つき	without equal	比類なく、ずぬけて
loud	（声が）大きい	without doubt	疑いなく
madam	お嬢さん	wits	知恵、機知、機転
noble	気高い、上品な	work	はたらかす

Q1 So, what you want is ＿＿＿＿＿＿＿＿＿＿＿＿＿＿＿＿＿．

Q2 「ノーブル」と名のつくものをあげてみよう。＿＿＿＿＿＿

　　　　（ちなみに我が家の近くにはパチンコ屋さんが．．．）

The Fox and the Stork

A Fox invited a Stork to dinner, at which the only fare provided was a large flat dish of soup. The Fox lapped it up with great relish, but the Stork with her long bill tried in vain to partake of the savory broth. Her evident distress caused the sly Fox much amusement.

But not long after the Stork invited him in turn, and set before him a pitcher with a long and narrow neck, into which she could get her bill with ease. Thus, while she enjoyed her dinner, the Fox sat by hungry and helpless, for it was impossible for him to reach the tempting contents of the vessel.

キツネとコウノトリ

　キツネがコウノトリを夕食に招待しました。そこで出された料理は、大きくて平べったい皿に入ったスープだけでした。キツネは大変喜んでピチャピチャとそれを平らげましたが、くちばしの長いコウノトリは、どんなにがんばってみてもおいしそうなスープを味わうことができませんでした。コウノトリが見るからに難儀している様子が、悪賢いキツネに非常な喜びを与えました。
　ですが、まもなくコウノトリはお返しにキツネを招待し、キツネの目の前に首が細くて長い水差しを置きました。そしてその中に、コウノトリは楽にくちばしを入れることができました。こうして、彼女が夕食を楽しむ間、キツネはお腹が空いてもどうすることもできなくて、ただ傍らに座っていました。なぜなら、彼にはおいしそうな器の中身に触れることができなかったからです。

****

the only fare (that was) provided 提供されたたったひとつの料理
tried in vain to partake of the savory broth
　　　　おいしいスープを飲もうとやってみたがだめだった
not long after 長いあとではなく、まもなく
a pitcher with a long and narrow neck, into which(=the pitcher) she could get her bill with ease   cf. she could get her bill into the pitcher with ease
it was impossible for him to … することは彼にはできませんでした

after	後に、あとで	large	大きな
amusement	楽しみ、楽しいこと	long	長い
before	〜の前に	much	たくさんの、多くの
bill	くちばし	narrow	細い、狭い
broth	スープ	neck	（ビンの）首
by	〜の傍らに、そばに	not	〜でない
cause	起こさせる	only	唯一の、たったひとつの
content	中身、内容物	partake of	〜を食べる
could	<can できる	pitcher	水差し、ピッチャー
dinner	夕食、正餐（さん）	provided	出された
dish	（料理の）一品	reach	〜に（手が）届く
distress	悩み、苦労、難儀	relish	with relish おいしそうに
ease	with ease 簡単に	sat	<sit by 脇に座っている
enjoy	楽しむ、味わう	savory	味の良い、おいしそうな
evident	明らかな、明白な	set	置く
fare	食物、料理	sly	悪賢い、老練な
flat	平らな	soup	スープ
for	〜なので	stork	コウノトリ
fox	キツネ	tempting	味覚をそそる
get into	入れる、届かせる	thus	こうして
great	とても、大変に	tried	<try 試す、試みる
helpless	お手上げで	turn	順番 in turn 今度は
hungry	お腹をすかせて	vain	in vain 無駄に
impossible	不可能な	vessel	器、容器
into	〜の中へ	was	<be 過去、単数
invite	招待する、招く	which	関係代名詞
lap up	ぴちゃぴちゃ飲む	while	〜の一方で

くちばしに赤ちゃんぶら下げて‥‥
おなじみのコウノトリさん。アニメなどでよく赤ん坊をくちばしにくわえて運んでくる姿を見かけますね。欧米ではそのように考えられています。そのコウノトリ、いろいろな種類のものがいるんだそうですが、日本古来のものは絶滅のおそれのある野生動植物に指定されています。なるほど、ここにも少子化の一因が‥‥

Q あなたは右の頬をたたかれたら、左の頬を差し出しますか？それとも、相手の頬をたたき返しますか。

The North Wind and the Sun

A dispute arose between the North Wind and the Sun, each claiming that he was stronger than the other. At last they agreed to try their powers upon a traveller, to see which could soonest strip him of his cloak.

The North Wind had the first try; and, gathering up all his force for the attack, he came whirling furiously down upon the man, and caught up his cloak as though he would wrest it from him by one single effort: but the harder he blew, the more closely the man wrapped it round himself.

Then came the turn of the Sun. At first he beamed gently upon the traveller, who soon unclasped his cloak and walked on with it hanging loosely about his shoulders: then he shone forth in his full strength, and the man, before he had gone many steps, was glad to throw his cloak right off and complete his journey more lightly clad.

Persuasion is better than force.

北風と太陽

　北風と太陽の間で、言い争いが起こりました。それぞれが自分の方が強いと言い張りました。最後に、2人は自分たちの力を旅人で試すことにしました。早く旅人の上着を脱がすことができた方が勝ちです。

　北風がまず挑戦しました。そして、攻撃のためにありったけの力をためると、男におそろしい勢いで吹き付けました。そして、上着をまくり上げました。あたかもひと吹きで上着を奪おうとするかのようでした。でも強く吹けば吹くほど、男はしっかりと上着で身を包みました。

　それから、太陽の番になりました。まず、太陽はやさしく旅人を照らしました。すると旅人はすぐに上着の前をはだけて、袖を通しただけのゆったりとした姿で歩き続けました。それから、太陽は力いっぱい輝きました。すると男は、たいして歩かないうちに、さっさと上着を脱いで身軽な装いで旅が続けられることを喜びました。

　説得は力にまさる。

****

the harder he blew, the more closely the man wrapped it round himself
　　　より強く吹けば吹くほど、よりしっかりと男は自分を上着でくるみました

about	〜のまわりに	journey	旅、旅行
agree	賛成する	last	at last ついに、結局
all	みな、すべての	loosely	ゆったりと
arose	<arise 起こる、生ずる	many	多くの
as though	あたかも〜のように	north	北の
attack	攻撃	one	ひとつの
beamed	<beam 輝く	other	他者、もう一方
before	〜の前に	persuasion	説得すること
better	<goodの比較	powers	力、強さ
between	〜のあいだ	right	まさに
blew	blow-blew-blown 吹く	round	〜のまわりに
by	〜によって	see	〜かどうかみる
came	come down upon 〜に襲いかかる	shone	<shine 輝く shine forth 輝き放つ
came the turn	順番がきた	shoulders	両肩
caught	<catch up まくり上げる	single	たった1つの
clad	lightly clad 薄着をして	soon	すぐに、早く
claiming	<claim 主張する	soonest	一番早く、一番はじめに
cloak	上着	steps	歩み、歩
closely	しっかりと	strength	力 in full strength 全力で
complete	完成させる	strip	脱がせる strip 人 of もの
could	<canの過去	stronger	より強い <strong
dispute	論争、言い争い	sun	太陽
each	それぞれ	then	それから、すると
effort	努力、奮闘	throw	throw off 脱ぎ捨てる
first	第1の、at first 最初は	traveller	旅人、旅行者
force	力	try	試みる、試み
full	いっぱいの、すべての	turn	順番
furiously	強く、おそろしく	unclasped	（ボタン、ひもを）解く
gathering	<gather up かき集める	upon	〜の上に
gently	やさしく	walked	<walk on 歩き続ける
glad	うれしい	whirling	渦巻きながら
gone	<go-went-gone	wind	風
had	<have	would	〜したかった
hanging	<hang かける、つるす	wrapped	<wrap くるむ、つつむ
harder	<hard 強い、はげしい	wrest	取り上げる

Q あなたは北風派、太陽派、それとも何派？

The Goose that Laid the Golden Eggs

 A Man and his Wife had the good fortune to possess a Goose which laid a Golden Egg every day. Lucky though they were, they soon began to think they were not getting rich fast enough, and, imagining the bird must be made of gold inside, they decided to kill it in order to secure the whole store of precious metal at once.
 But when they cut it open they found it was just like any other goose. Thus, they neither got rich all at once, as they had hoped, nor enjoyed any longer the daily addition to their wealth.
 Much wants more and loses all.

金の卵を生むガチョウ

 ある夫婦が、毎日１つ金の卵を生むガチョウを飼う、という幸運に恵まれました。運がよかったにもかかわらず、すぐに２人は金持ちになるスピードが十分ではないと思い始め、その鳥のお腹の中も金でできているに違いないと想像して、ありったけの金（きん）を即座に手に入れるために、ガチョウをすぐ殺すことに決めました。
 ですが、その鳥のお腹を開けてみると、何ら他のガチョウと変わるところはありませんでした。こういうわけで、望んだように一夜にして大金持ちになることもできませんでしたし、一日一日自分たちの蓄えが増えていくのを楽しむことも、２人にはもはやできませんでした。
 欲張りすぎるとすべてを失う（多いことは、より多くを求め、そしてすべてを失う）。

****

a Goose (←which laid a Golden Egg) 金の卵を生んだガチョウ
lucky though they were = though they were lucky　運がよかったにもかかわらず
they soon began to think ‥ A ‥, and, imagining ‥ B ‥, they decided ‥ C ‥.
彼らはすぐにAと考え始め、そして、（Bと想像したために、）Cすることを決めました
just like any other goose　他のどんなガチョウをとってみてもちょうど同じ
they neither (got rich) … nor (enjoyed … the daily addition)
　　　　　　金持ちにもなれなかったし、毎日増えるのを楽しむこともできなかった

  Q1　あなたは「金の卵を生むガチョウ」を飼って（持って）
  　　いますか？　それはなんですか？
  Q2　欲張り過ぎて失敗した経験はありますか？

addition	増加、増えること	loses	<lose 失う、なくす
all	すべて	lucky	幸運な
all at once	すぐさま、たちどころに	made	<make
any	いかなる	man	a man and his wife 夫婦
not any longer	もはや〜ではない	metal	金属
as	〜のように	more	より多く
began	<begin to 〜し始める	much	多く、多量
bird	鳥	must	〜にちがいない
but	しかし	neither A nor B	AでもBでもない
cut	切る cut open 切り開く	not	〜ない
daily	日々の、毎日の	once	at once すぐに、即座に
day	every day 毎日	open	開いた
decided	<decide 決心する	order	in order to 〜するために
egg	卵	other	他の
enjoyed	<enjoy 楽しむ	possess	持つ、所有する
enough	十分に	precious	貴重な
fast	早く		precious stone 貴金属、金
fortune	good fortune 幸運	secure	確保する、手に入れる
found	<find 見つける、分かる	soon	すぐに、まもなく
getting	<get rich 金持になる	store	蓄え、貯蔵品
gold	金 made of gold 金製の	that	関係代名詞
golden	金の	think	思う、考える
goose	ガチョウ	though	〜ではあるが
got	<get 〜になる	thus	こうして
had	<have 持つ、飼う； 過去完了を作る	wants	<want 欲する、求める
		was	<be, 過去単数
hoped	<hope 望む、希望する	wealth	富、財産
imagining	<imagine 想像する、思う	were	<be, 過去複数
inside	内側	when	〜の時
just	ちょうど	which	関係代名詞
kill	殺す	whole	すべての、全部の
laid	<lay an egg 卵を生む	wife	妻
like	〜のように		

この木なんの木 . . .

Money doesn't grow on trees. 「金のなる木はない」というのが相場ですが、やっぱり、ゆすると金が落ちてくるという伝説の money tree や、cash cow など、いろんな表現がありますね、英語にも。ほら日本語にも、金づる、とかネ。

Three Little Pigs

There was an old sow with three little pigs, and as she had not enough to keep them, she sent them out to seek their fortune. The first that went off met a man with a bundle of straw, and said to him:

"Please, man, give me that straw to build me a house."

Which the man did, and the little pig built a house with it. Presently came along a wolf, and knocked at the door, and said:

"Little pig, little pig, let me come in."

To which the pig answered:

"No, no, by the hair of my chinny chin chin."

The wolf then answered to that:

"Then I'll huff, and I'll puff, and I'll blow your house in."

So he huffed, and he puffed, and he blew his house in, and ate up the little pig.

3匹の子豚

　3人の子どもがいる年配のお母さん豚がおりましたが、子どもたちを食べさせていくには十分ではなかったので、自分で生きていくようにと、子どもたちを世の中に送り出すことにしました。最初に出て行った子は、わらの束を持った男に出会い、言いました。「お願いです、おじさん。僕の家を作るのにそのわらをください」すると、男はわらをくれました。そして子豚はそれで家を建てました。やがて、オオカミがやってきて、玄関をノックして言いました。「子豚ちゃん、子豚ちゃん、中へ入れてちょうだい」それに、子豚は答えました。「やだよ、やだよ、絶対ヤーダ」すると、それに対してオオカミが答えました。「それじゃ、ヒー、フー、とやってお前の家を吹き壊してやる」そしてオオカミはヒー、フー、とやって家を吹き壊し、子豚をすっかり平らげてしまいました。

三匹の子豚（1）　19

along	come along やって来る	little	小さな、かわいい
answered	<answer 答える	man	男の人
as	～なので	met	< meet 会う、出会う
ate	< eat up 食べ尽くす、平らげる	no	いやだ、否
blew	blow-blew-blown	off	go off 出かける、出発する
blow	blow in ～を吹き飛ばす	old	年老いた、年配の
build	建てる build-built-built	out	send out 送り出す
bundle	束、束ねたもの	pig	豚
by	～にかけて、誓って	please	どうか、どうぞ
came	来た come-came-come	presently	やがて、まもなく
chin	あご	puff	フーと吹く
chinny	あごの先が目だつ	said	<say-said-said 言う
come	come in 中へ入る	seek	求める、探す
did	do-did-done する、行う	seek one's fortune 成功の道を求める	
door	ドア、玄関	sent	< send out 送り出す
enough	十分な、十分に	so	そして
first	最初の（子豚）	sow	雌の豚、お母さん豚
fortune	幸運、しあわせ	straw	わら、麦わら
give	与える	that	あの、関係代名詞
had	<have 持つ、所有する	then	すると、それから、それなら
hair	髪、ヒゲ	There was	～に…がいました
house	家	three	3匹の
huff	ヒューヒュー吹く	to	～するための、～に対して
I'll	<I will 私は～する	went	< go-went-gone
keep	養う、育てる	which	関係代名詞
knocked	<knock at ～をノックする	with	～を持った、～を利用して
let	～させる	wolf	オオカミ

had not enough = did not have enough
the first [pig](that went off) 最初のブタは（←出かけた）＝最初に出かけたブタは
build me a house 自分の（ために）家を建てる
which the man did （そのこと［わらをくれること］を男は行った＝男はわらをくれた
To which the pig answered 　（そのこと［入れてちょうだい］に対して）答えた
no, by the hair of chinny chin chin 絶対いやだ
　　　　　　　　　　　（なぜこう言うのかはよくわからない）

20 Three Little Pigs(2)

The second little pig met a man with a bundle of furze, and said:
"Please, man, give me that furze to build a house."
Which the man did, and the pig built his house. Then along came the wolf, and said:
"Little pig, little pig, let me come in."
"No, no, by the hair of my chinny chin chin."
"Then I'll puff, and I'll huff, and I'll blow your house in."
So he huffed, and he puffed, and he puffed, and he huffed, and at last he blew the house down, and he ate up the little pig.

The third little pig met a man with a load of bricks, and said:
"Please, man, give me those bricks to build a house with."
So the man gave him the bricks, and he built his house with them. So the wolf came, as he did to the other little pigs, and said:
"Little pig, little pig, let me come in."
"No, no, by the hair of my chinny chin chin."
"Then I'll huff, and I'll puff, and I'll blow your house in."

　2番目の子豚は、ハリエニシダの枝の束を持った男に出会い、言いました。「お願いです、おじさん。僕の家を作るのにそのハリエニシダをください」男はハリエニシダをくれました。そして子豚は自分の家を建てました。すると、例のオオカミがやってきて言いました。「子豚ちゃん、子豚ちゃん、中へ入れてちょうだい」「やだよ、やだよ、絶対ヤーダ」「それじゃ、ヒー、フー、とやってお前の家を吹き壊してやる」そしてオオカミは、ヒー、フー、フー、ヒー、とやってついに家を吹き倒し、子豚をすっかり平らげてしまいました。

　3匹目の子豚は、レンガをたくさん持った人に出会い、言いました。「お願いです、おじさん。僕の家を作るのにそのレンガをください」男はレンガをくれました。そして子豚はレンガで自分の家を建てました。すると、ほかの子豚のところに来たように、例のオオカミがやってきて言いました。「子豚ちゃん、子豚ちゃん、中へ入れてちょうだい」「やだよ、やだよ、絶対ヤーダ」「それじゃ、ヒー、フー、とやってお前の家を吹き壊してやる」

along	come along やって来る	furze	ハリエニシダ
as	〜のように	gave	give-gave-given
at last	ついに、結局	I'll	I will
ate	<eat up 平らげる	let me come in	私を中へ入れてくれ
blew	<blow	load	a load of たくさんの〜
bricks	レンガ	other	ほかの
bundle	束、束ねたもの	second	2番目の
came	<come	third	3番目の
down	blow down 吹き壊す	those	<that

along came the wolf = the wolf came along　（オオカミがやってきた）

〜を持った人
　　a man with a bundle of straw　　わらの束を持った人
　　　　　　　a bundle of furze　　ハリエニシダの束を持った人
　　　　　　　a load of bricks　　レンガの山を持った人

as he did to the other little pigs
　　　　　　　　= as he came to the (two) other little pigs

＊興味のある人は、ハリエニシダがどんな植物か、調べてみましょう。

＊レンガの家の様子を描いてみましょう。

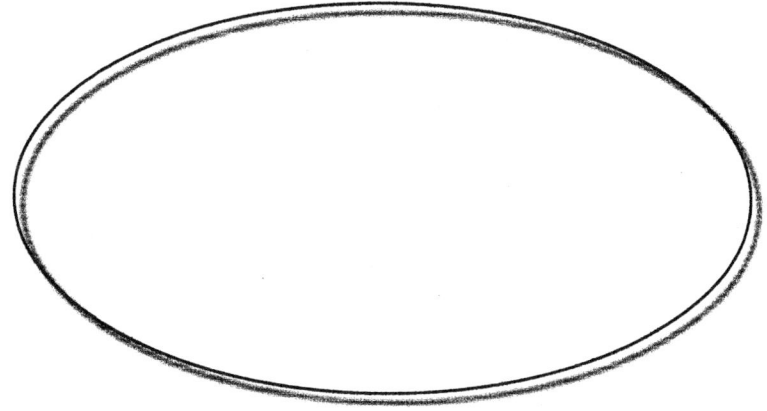

22 The Three Little Pigs(3)

Well, he huffed, and he puffed, and he huffed and he puffed, and he puffed and huffed; but he could not get the house down. When he found that he could not, with all his huffing and puffing, blow the house down, he said:
"Little pig, I know where there is a nice field of turnips."
"Where?" said the little pig.
"Oh, in Mr. Smith's Home-field, and if you will be ready tomorrow morning I will call for you, and we will go together, and get some for dinner."
"Very well," said the little pig, "I will be ready. What time do you mean to go?"
"Oh, at six o'clock."

Well, the little pig got up at five, and got the turnips before the wolf came (which he did about six) and who said:
"Little Pig, are you ready?"
The little pig said: "Ready! I have been and come back again, and got a nice potful for dinner."
The wolf felt very angry at this, but thought that he would be up to the little pig somehow or other, so he said:

　さて、オオカミはヒー、フー、ヒー、フー、フー、ヒー、とやりましたが、家を壊すことはできませんでした。どんなにヒー、フーとやっても家を壊すことができないのが分かると、オオカミは言いました。「子豚ちゃん、よいかぶの畑の場所知ってるんだ」「どこ」と子豚は言いました。「えっとー、スミスさんちの家の畑。明日の朝いっしょに行きたければ呼びに来るよ。いっしょに行って夕食用に手に入れようよ」「いいですねー」と子豚が言いました。「待ってます。何時に来ますか」「えっと、6時だね」
　さて、子豚は5時に起きて、オオカミが来る前にかぶを手に入れました。オオカミは6時ごろに来て、言いました。「子豚ちゃん、行きましょう」子豚は答えました。「行きましょう、だって！もう行って帰ってきたところだよ。夕飯においしそうなやつ、鍋に一杯ね」これにはオオカミもたいへん腹を立てましたが、どうにかこうにかして子豚をやっつけてやろうと考え、言いました。

****

get the house down　家を壊す
blow the house down　家を吹き壊す
with all his huffing and puffing　どんなにヒーフーと吹いても

三匹の子豚（３）

about	～ごろ	nice	素晴らしい、おいしい
again	再び、また	not	～でない
all	with all ～にもかかわらず	o'clock	～時
angry at	～におこって	of	～の
are	\<be	oh	おお、あのう
at	～時に	or	～か、あるいは
back	come back もどる	potful	鍋一杯の
be, been	\<be動詞 原形、過去分詞	ready	準備、用意ができた
before	～する前に	six	6
call for	～を呼びに寄る	some	いくらか、すこし
came	\<come	somehow or other	なんとかして
could	\<can 過去	that	（接続詞）～と
dinner	夕食	there is	～に...がある
felt	\<feel 感ずる	this	このこと
field	畑	thought	\<think 思う、考える
five	5	time	what time 何時
for	～のために、用に	together	いっしょに
found	\<find 分かる、見つける	tomorrow	明日
get	手に入れる、～にする	turnip	かぶ
got	\<get up 起きる	up to	～に対抗する
have	現在完了を作る	very	とても
	have been 行ってきたところ	well	よい、ええと
homefield	家の畑	when	～の時
home	家	where	～のところ（関係詞）、どこ
if	もし～なら	which	そのこと（関係詞）
know	知っている	who	そしてその人が（関係詞）
mean to	～するつもりだ	will	～でしょう would（過去）
morning	朝		

I know [where there is a nice field] (よい畑のあるところ)を知っている
which he did about 6　それ（＝迎えに来ること）を彼は6時ごろにやりました
I have been and come back =I have been to the field and I have come back

"Little pig, I know where there is a nice apple-tree."
"Where?" said the pig.
"Down at Merry-garden," replied the wolf, "and if you will not deceive me I will come for you, at five o'clock tomorrow and get some apples."

Well, the little pig bustled up the next morning at four o'clock, and went off for the apples, hoping to get back before the wolf came; but he had further to go, and had to climb the tree, so that just as he was coming down from it, he saw the wolf coming, which, as you may suppose, frightened him very much. When the wolf came up he said:
"Little pig, what! are you here before me? Are they nice apples?"
"Yes, very," said the little pig. "I will throw you down one."
And he threw it so far, that, while the wolf was gone to pick it up, the little pig jumped down and ran home. The next day the wolf came again, and said to the little pig:
"Little pig, there is a fair at Shanklin this afternoon, will you go?"
"Oh yes," said the pig, "I will go; what time shall you be ready?"

「子豚ちゃん、おいしいリンゴの木のありか、知ってるんだ」「どこ」と子豚が言いました。「メリーガーデン（楽しいお庭）のところだよ」とオオカミが答えました。「それで、もし今度は私のことをだまさないって言うなら、迎えに来よう。明日の朝5時だよ。リンゴを取りにいこう」
　さて子豚は、オオカミがやって来る前に帰って来ようと思って、翌朝4時に飛び起きて、リンゴを取りに行きました。ですが、道のりは思ったよりも遠く、木にも登らなければならなかったので、リンゴの木から降りようとしていると、ちょうどオオカミがやって来るのが見えました。それは、皆さんお分かりでしょう、とてもおそろしいことでした。オオカミはやって来ると言いました。「子豚ちゃん、なんだい。僕よりも先にここに来たのかい。リンゴはおいしいかい」「うん、とっても」と子豚は言いました。「ひとつ投げ降ろしてあげるよ」そして子豚はとても遠くへと投げ、オオカミが拾いに行っている間に、木から飛び降りて走って家へと帰りました。翌日、またオオカミがやって来て子豚に言いました。「子豚ちゃん、今日の午後、シャンクリンで縁日があるんだ。行くかい」「うん、行く」と子豚は言いました。「ぼく、行くよ。何時になったら行くの」

三匹の子豚（４）

afternoon	午後	get back	帰宅する
apple	リンゴ	go	行く >gone
apple-tree	リンゴの木	here	ここに
as	～の時に、～のように	hope to	～と願って
at	～で	jump	飛ぶ
before	～の前に	just as	ちょうど～のように
bustle up	急ぐ	may	～かもしれない
but	しかし	Merry-garden [地名]メリーガーデン
came	<come	much	大変に
climb	登る	next	次の
come	come up 近づく	off	go off 出発する
	come down 降りる	one	（リンゴ）１個
day	日　the next day 翌日	pick up	拾う
deceive	だます	ran	<run 走る
down	下へ、～のところに	replied	<reply 返事をする
fair	市、縁日	Shanklin	[地名]シャンクリン
far	遠くへ	so	とても
five	5	some	いくつかの
four	4	suppose	思う、仮定する
frighten	驚かす	that	(so) that とても～なので...
from	～から	threw	<throw 投げる
further	<farの比較級	tomorrow	明日
garden	庭	tree	木

I know [where there is a nice apple-tree](よいリンゴの木のある場所を)知っている
he had further to go　（思ったよりも）もっと遠くへ行かなければならなかった
just as he was coming down from it, he saw the wolf coming
ちょうどそれから降りてこようとしていた時に、オオカミが来るのを見た
the little pig bustled up the next morning at four o'clock 子豚は飛び起き 翌朝４時に
and went off for the apples, 出発した、リンゴ（を取る）ために
hoping to get back before the wolf came; オオカミが来る前に戻ることを望んで
but he had further to go, しかし彼は、さらなる道のりをもっていた、行くべき
and had to climb the tree, しなければならなかった、木に登ることを
so that just as he was coming down from it, その結果、ちょうど降りようとした時
he saw the wolf coming, 彼は見た、オオカミが来るのを　　　Lそれから
which, そのことが（オオカミが来たことが）
as you may suppose, ～ように、あなたが思うかもしれない
frightened him very much こわがらせた、彼を、とても

"At three," said the wolf. So the little pig went off before the time as usual, and got to the fair, and bought a butter-churn, which he was going home with, when he saw the wolf coming. Then he could not tell what to do. So he got into the churn to hide, and by so doing turned it round, and it rolled down the hill with the pig in it, which frightened the wolf so much, that he ran home without going to the fair. He went to the little pig's house, and told him how frightened he had been by a great round thing which came down the hill past him. Then the little pig said:
"Hah, I frightened you, then. I had been to the fair and bought a butter-churn, and when I saw you, I got into it, and rolled down the hill."

Then the wolf was very angry indeed, and declared he would eat up the little pig, and that he would get down the chimney after him. When the little pig saw what he was about, he hung on the pot full of water, and made up a blazing fire, and, just as the wolf was coming down, took off the cover, and in fell the wolf; so the little pig put on the cover again in an instant, boiled him up, and ate him for supper, and lived happy ever afterwards.

「3時」とオオカミは言いました。そうして、いつものように、子豚は早く出かけ、縁日に着いて、バターを作るかく乳機を買いました。それを持って帰ろうとしていると、オオカミがやってくるのが目に入りました。その時、子豚はどうしたらいいのか分かりませんでした。そこで子豚は隠れるために、かく乳機に潜り込んで、そして中に入ったままかく乳機を倒すと、それは子豚を入れたままゴロゴロと丘をころがり落ちていき、オオカミはその様子を見てとても驚いてしまい、縁日には行かず家へと走って帰りました。オオカミは子豚の家へ行くと、自分のそばを転がり落ちていったその大きな丸いものに、どんなに驚いたか話しました。すると子豚が言いました。「えへー、それじゃ、ぼくあなたのこと驚かしちゃったんだね。ぼく、縁日に行って、かく乳機買ったんだ。で、君を見た時、その中に入って丘を転がり落ちたの」
　すると、オオカミは本当にたいへん腹を立て、煙突から降りて子豚を捕まえ、食べてやる、と言い放ちました。子豚はオオカミがしようとしていることを見て取ると、水をいっぱいに入れた鍋を掛け、燃え立つ火をおこし、そしてまさにオオカミが降りて来るその時に、鍋のふたを取って、オオカミは鍋の中に落ちました。そして子豚は素早くまたふたを閉め、オオカミをすっかりと茹で上げ、夕食に食べてしまい、それからずっと幸せに暮らしました。

about	〜しようとしている	indeed	本当に、まったく
after	〜のあとを追いかけて	instant	in an instant すぐに
afterwards	その後、それ以降	into	get into 〜の中へ入る
again	また、再び	just as	ちょうど〜の時に
angry	怒っている	lived	<live happy 幸せに暮らす
before	〜の前に	made	make up a fire 火をおこす
blazing	赤々と燃え立つ	off	take off 〜を取る
boiled	<boil up ゆで上げる	on	put on 付ける、かぶせる
bought	<buy 買う	past	〜を通り過ぎて
butter-churn	バターを作るかく乳機	pot	なべ、つぼ、かめ
chimney	煙突	ran	<run home 走って家へ帰る
churn	かく乳機	rolled	<roll down ころがり落ちる
cover	(鍋の) ふた	round	ぐるりと; 丸い
declared	<declare 宣言する	supper	for supper 夕食に
ever	ずっと	tell	分かる、言える
fell	<fall 落ちる	then	それじゃ;その時、それから
fire	火	thing	もの
frightened	<frighten 驚かせる	three	at three 3時に
full of	〜でいっぱいの	told	<tell ... how どんなに...か話す
get down	降りる	took	<take off 〜を取る
got	<get to 〜に到着する	turned	<turn round 〜をまわす
great	大きな	usual	as usual いつも通りに
had	過去完了を作る	was	<be
hah	はあ、ほう	water	水
hide	隠れる	went	<go off 出発する
hill	丘	what to do	何をすべきか
how frightened	どんなに驚いたか	without	〜せずに
hung	<hang on 〜をつるす		

got to the fair (市に着き), and bought a butter-churn (そしてかく乳機を買い), which he was going home with (そしてそれとともに家へ帰ろうとしていたが＝持って帰ろうとしていたが), when he saw the wolf coming (するとその時にオオカミが来るのが見えた).
Then he could not tell what to do. するとその時、何をすべきかわからなかった
it rolled down the hill with the pig in it
　　　　それ(＝かく乳機)は丘を転がり落ちた、ブタを入れた状態で

The Bremen Town-Musicians

A certain man had a donkey, which had carried the corn-sacks to the mill indefatigably for many a long year; but his strength was going, and he was growing more and more unfit for work. Then his master began to consider how he might best save his keep; but the donkey, seeing that no good wind was blowing, ran away and set out on the road to Bremen. "There," he thought, "I can surely be town-musician."

When he had walked some distance, he found a hound lying on the road, gasping like one who had run till he was tired. "What are you gasping so for, you big fellow?" asked the donkey.

"Ah," replied the hound, "as I am old, and daily grow weaker, and no longer can hunt, my master wanted to kill me, so I took to flight; but now how am I to earn my bread?"

ブレーメンの音楽隊

　ある男がロバを飼っておりました。そのロバは、長い年月疲れ知らずで、小麦粉の袋を粉挽き場へと運んでいました。ですが、しだいに力が出なくなってきて、だんだんと仕事に向かなくなってきました。するとロバの飼い主は、どうやったら餌を節約できるか、と考え始めました。ですが、ロバは風向きが悪くなってきた気配を感じると、逃げ出してブレーメンへの道を歩み始めました。「そこでなら」と彼は思いました、「僕はきっと街の楽団員になれるよ」
　しばらく歩くと、ロバは猟犬が道に寝そべっているのに気付きました。疲れるまで走り通した人のようにハアハアあえいでいました。「何をそんなにあえいでおいでですか、おっきなお方」とロバはたずねました。
　「ええ」と猟犬は返事をしました、「年をとって毎日毎日弱っていくので、もう狩りもできなくなりまして、ご主人様が私を殺したがっていたものですから、逃げ出しました。でもこうなった今、どうやって食べ物を手に入れたらいいんでしょうか」

ブレーメンの音楽隊（1）

a certain man	ある男	many a long year	長年
be to	〜すべき、したらよい	master	飼い主、ご主人
as	〜なので	might	<may best
ask	たずねる		どうやったら一番〜できるか
began	<begin 始める	mill	製粉場、水車小屋
blow	（風が）吹く	more and more	いっそう〜
bread	パン、食事	no longer	もはや〜ない
Bremen	（地名）ブレーメン	ran	<run away 逃げる
carried	<carry 運ぶ、運搬する	replied	<reply 返事をする
consider	考える、考慮する	road	道 on the road 途中で
corn-sack	小麦の入った袋	save	節約する、とっておく
daily	毎日、日々	seeing that	〜と分かると
distance	距離	set out	出発する
donkey	ロバ	so	そんなに；だから
earn	かせぐ	strength	力、体力
fellow	ひと、やつ	surely	きっと、確かに
flight	take to flight 逃げる	then	すると
found	<find 見つける	there	そこで
gasp	ハアハア息をする	thought	<think 考える
go	無くなる、弱くなる	till	〜まで
grow	〜になる	tired	疲れた
hound	猟犬、犬	town-musician	街の音楽家、楽団員
how	いかに、どうやって	unfit	適さない、不向きな
hunt	狩をする、獲物を捕え	walk	歩く
indefatigably	疲れ知らずで	want	〜したい
keep	飼料、えさ	weaker	<weak、弱い
kill	殺す	wind	風、気配
like	〜のように	work	仕事、働くこと
lying	<lie 横になる、横たわる	year	年
look in	のぞき込む		

many a 単数名詞という（古い）表現がある
save his keep えさを節約する
he found a hound lying 犬が寝っ転がっているのを見つけた
gasping like one (←who had run) 走った人のようにあえいでいる

cornはいつもトウモロコシとは限りません。要注意。
　（ちなみにアイスクリームの「コーン」は円錐：別の単語です）

"I tell you what," said the donkey, "I am going to Bremen, and shall be town-musician there; go with me and engage yourself also as a musician. I will play the lute, and you shall beat the kettledrum."

The hound agreed, and on they went.

Before long they came to a cat, sitting on the path, with a face like three rainy days! "Now then, old shaver, what has gone askew with you?" asked the donkey.

"Who can be merry when his neck is in danger?" answered the cat. "Because I am now getting old, and my teeth are worn to stumps, and I prefer to sit by the fire and spin, rather than hunt about after mice, my mistress wanted to drown me, so I ran away. But now good advice is scarce. Where am I to go?"

"Go with us to Bremen. You understand night-music, you can be a town-musician."

「いいこと、お教えしましょう」とロバが言いました。「私はブレーメンへ行くところです。そこで街の楽団員になることにしました。いっしょに行ってあなたも楽団員になってみませんか。私はリュートを演奏します。あなたはティンパニーをおやりなさい」

猟犬は賛成し、2人は先へと進みました。

やがて、2人はネコに出会いました。細道に座っていて、3日も雨降りが続いたような顔をしていました。「さてさて、ご老体、どうなさいましたかな」とロバがたずねました。

「首があぶねえって時に、安閑としてられるやつがいるかい」とネコが答えました。「年をとってきたんでねえ、歯が鈍くなっちまってよ。おまけに火の側に座って糸車回してる方がよくなっちまったんだよ。ネズミを追っかけるよりも。そんなもんで、女飼い主様があたしを溺れさせようってんだ。だから逃げてきたのよ。でもなあ、こうなっちまっちゃ、いい知恵はでねえってもんよ。どこへ行ったらいいもんかなあ」

「いっしょにブレーメンへ行きましょう。あなたは夜の音楽に造詣が深いから、街の楽団員になれますよ」

about	あちこちと	mice	<mouse ネズミ
advice	助言、アドバイス	mistress	女主人、女飼い主
after	〜を追い求めて	musician	音楽家
agree	賛成する	neck	首
also	もまた	night-music	夜の音楽
answer	答える	now then	さてさて
as	〜として	old shaver	ご老体、お年寄り
askew	ゆがんで、まずくなって	path	小道、細道
beat	たたく	play	演奏する
because	〜なので	prefer to	〜するのを好む
before long	そのうちに、やがて	rainy	雨降りの
by the fire	火のそばに	rather than	〜よりむしろ
cat	ネコ	scarce	少ない、めずらしい
drown	溺れさせる	shall	〜するつもりだ
engage oneself	従事する	shaver	そる人、ヤツ
face	顔、顔つき	sit	腰をおろす、座る
fire	火、暖炉	spin	糸車を回して糸を紡ぐ
get	〜になる	stump	切り株、根っこ
go askew	まずいことになる	teeth	<tooth 歯
in danger	危険な、危ない	tell you what	いいですか
kettledrum	ティンパニー	understand	分かる、理解する
lute	リュート	went	<go on 進む、行く
merry	陽気な、楽しい	worn	<wear すり減らす

(I) shall be town-musician 街の音楽家になるんだ（そう決めたんだ）
on they went = they went on 彼らは歩みを進めました
I prefer to sit by the fire and spin, 私は火のそばに座って糸を紡ぐ方が好きだ
rather than hunt about after mice ネズミをあちこち追いかけ回すよりも
Where am I to go? 私はどこへ行くべきか

The cat thought well of it, and went with them. After this the three fugitives came to a farm-yard, where a cock was sitting upon the gate, crowing with all his might. "Your crow goes through and through one," said the donkey. "What is the matter?"

"I have been foretelling fine weather, because it is the day on which Our Lady washes the Christ-child's little shirts, and wants to dry them," said the cock; "but guests are coming for Sunday, so the housewife has no pity, and has told the cook that she intends to eat me in the soup to-morrow, and this evening I am to have my head cut off. Now I am crowing at full pitch while I can."

"Ah, but red-comb," said the donkey, "you had better come away with us. We are going to Bremen; you can find something better than death everywhere: you have a good voice, and if we make music together it must have some quality!"

　それはいい考えだと思い、ネコはいっしょに行きました。この後、3人の逃亡者は農場の庭へたどり着きました。すると門柱の上には雄鶏が座っていて、声を限りに鳴いていました。「あなたの鳴き声は体中に響きますね」とロバが言いました。「一体どうしたんですか」
　「私はずっと晴天の予報を出していたんです。だってマリア様が幼児キリストのかわいらしいシャツをお洗いになる日ですから、乾かしたいでしょう」と雄鶏が言いました、「でも日曜にはお客様がみえるんです。で、おかみさんは情け容赦なくって、明日私をスープに入れて食べるつもりだって、料理係に言うんです。ですから、今晩首を切られちゃうんですよ。だから今のうちに声を限りに歌ってるんです」
　「そう、でもね、赤いトサカさん」とロバはいいました「私たちといっしょに行ったらいいですよ。私たちはブレーメンへ行くところなんです。どこへ行ったって死ぬよりはましですよ。あなたはいい声をお持ちですね、ですからいっしょに音楽をやればきっといいものができますよ」

ブレーメンの音楽隊（3） 33

after	〜の後	might	力
be to	〜することになっている		with all his might 力の限り
better	<good	must	〜にちがいない
Christ-child	幼児キリスト	one	ひと
cock	雄鶏、おんどり	Our Lady	マリア様、聖母マリア
come away	逃げる	pitch	（声の）高さ
cook	コック、料理人		at full pitch 大声を張り上げて
crow	（雄鶏の）鳴き声；鳴く	pity	哀れみ、情け、同情
cut off	切り落とす	quality	質が良いこと、良質
death	死、死ぬこと	red-comb	とさか
dry	乾かす、干す	said	<say 言う
eat	食べる	shirt	シャツ、肌着
evening	夕方、夕べ	sit upon	〜の上に座る
everywhere	どこでも	some	何らかの、いくらかの
farm-yard	（農家、農場の）庭	something	何か、あるもの
fine	すばらしい	soup	スープ
foretell	予言する、予報する	Sunday	日曜日
fugitive	逃亡者	thought	<think well of
gate	門、門柱		〜をよく思う
go through	体中に響く	to-morrow=tomorrow	明日
guest	お客さん	together	いっしょに
had better	〜するほうがよい	told	<tell 話す、言う
have my head cut off		voice	声
	首を切り落とされる	wash	洗う、洗濯する
housewife	主婦、おかみさん	weather	天気
intend	〜するつもりだ	while I can	= while I can crow
matter	What is the matter?		（死ぬ前に）できるだけ（大声
	どうしましたか		で鳴く）

came to a farm-yard, where a cock was sitting upon the gate
農場の庭へと来ました。そしてそこでは、門の上に雄鶏が座っていました
　　　　　　　↑crowing with all his might すべての力を出して鳴きながら
it is the day on which 〜する日
I am to have my head cut off 頭（日本語では首）を切り落とされることに決まって
いる：　　be to（運命）＋　have 目的語　＋　過去分詞（〜される）
you can find something better than death everywhere
なにかを見いだせる　死より何かよいものを　どこででも

The cock agreed to this plan, and all four went on together. They could not, however, reach the city of Bremen in one day, and in the evening they came to a forest where they meant to pass the night. The donkey and the hound laid themselves down under a large tree, the cat and the cock settled themselves in the branches; but the cock flew right to the top, where he was most safe. Before he went to sleep he looked round on all four sides, and thought he saw in the distance a little spark burning; so he called out to his companions that there must be a house not far off, for he saw a light. The donkey said, "If so, we had better get up and go on, for the shelter here is bad." The hound thought that a few bones with some meat on would do him good too!

So they made their way to the place where the light was, and soon saw it shine brighter and grow larger, until they came to a well-lighted robber's house. The donkey, as the biggest, went to the window and looked in.

　雄鶏はこの計画に賛成し、4人みんなで進んで行きました。ですが、彼らは一日でブレーメンへたどり着くことはできませんでした。夕方になると、そこで一夜を過ごそうかという森へとやって来ました。ロバと猟犬は大きな木の根元で横になり、ネコと雄鶏は枝の上に落ち着きました。ですが、雄鶏はずっと木の天辺まで飛んで行きました。なぜならそこが一番安全だったからです。眠りにつく前に雄鶏が四方を見回してみると、遠くに小さな火が燃えているのを見たように思いました。そこで彼は仲間たちにそう遠くないところに家があるに違いない、と叫びました。だって明かりが見えたんですから。ロバが言いました。「そうなら、起きて先へ進んだ方がよさそうだ。ここはあまり夜露がしのげないから」猟犬は、ちょっと肉の付いた骨が2、3本あったら元気も出るのに、と思いました。
　こうして彼らは明かりのある場所へと歩みを進め、まもなく明かりがより明るく、大きくなるのを目にし、やがて彼らは明々と火のともった泥棒の家へとやって来ました。ロバは一番大きいので、窓のところへ行き、のぞき込みました。

ブレーメンの音楽隊（４）　35

as the biggest	1番大きいものとして	make one's way to	〜へと進む
bad	悪い、よくない	meant	mean to 〜するつもり
before	〜の前に	meat	肉
bone	骨	with some meat on	少し肉がついた
branch	枝	must	〜にちがいない
bright	明るい	pass the night	一夜を過ごす
burn	燃える	place	場所
call	大声で呼ぶ、呼びかける	plan	計画
city	市、都市	reach	着く、到着する
companion	仲間、連れ	right	ちょうど、ずっと
distance	遠距離、遠いところ	robber	泥棒
do ... good	役に立つ、効果がある	safe	安全な
far off	遠くはなれた	saw	<see 見る
few	a few 2、3の	settle oneself	落ち着く、くつろぐ
flew	<fly 飛ぶ	shelter	夜露をしのぐ場所、宿
for	〜なので	shine	光る、輝く
forest	森	sleep	go to sleep 眠る
four sides	四方	spark	火花、火の粉
get up	起き上がる	together	いっしょに、ともに
go on	先へ進む	too	その上、おまけに
grow	〜になる	top	一番上、天辺
however	しかしながら	tree	木
if so	もしそうなら	under	〜の下に
in one day	1日のうちに、1日で	until	〜まで
laid	<lay oneself down 横たわる	well-lighted	照明のついた、明るい
large	大きな	window	窓
light	明かり、光	would	<will 過去、だったろう
look round	見回す		

he saw (in the distance) a little spark burning
遠くに小さな火が燃えているのを見た
there must be a house not far off
遠く離れたところではないところに家があるに違いない
they made their way to the place (where the light was)
彼らは（明かりがあった→）場所へと進んだ

The Bremen Town-Musicians(5)

"What do you see, my grey-horse?" asked the cock. "What do I see?" answered the donkey; "a table covered with good things to eat and drink, and robbers sitting at it enjoying themselves." "That would be the sort of thing for us," said the cock. "Yes, yes; ah, how I wish we were there!" said the donkey.

Then the animals took counsel together how they should manage to drive away the robbers, and at last they thought of a plan. The donkey was to place himself with his fore-feet upon the window-ledge, the hound was to jump on the donkey's back, the cat was to climb upon the dog, and lastly the cock was to fly up and perch upon the head of the cat.

「どうだい、あし毛馬君」雄鶏がききました。「どうかって」ロバが答えました。「おいしそうな食べ物と飲み物がいっぱいの食卓だよ。それに、泥棒たちが席に着いて楽しくやってるよ」「それはぼくたちにおあつらえ向きだな」雄鶏が言いました。「そう、そう。もう、あっちへ行きたいなあ！」ロバが言いました。

そこで動物たちはどうやったら泥棒たちを追っ払えるか、いっしょに話し合い、ついに計画ができ上がりました。ロバが前足を窓枠に掛けて立ち、猟犬がロバの背中に飛び上がり、ネコが猟犬の背中に駆け上がり、最後には雄鶏が飛び上がってネコの頭に止まることになりました。

****

a table covered with ↓　　　　↓でおおわれたテーブル
　　good things to eat and drink　食べたり飲んだりするためによいもの
robbers sitting at it enjoying themselves
　　　楽しみながら、食事の席に着いている、泥棒たち
how I wish we were there 私たちがそこにいたら、どんなにいいだろうか
took counsel together how ～するにはどうしたらいいかと相談した
manage to drive away the robbers 泥棒たちをなんとか追い払う

ブレーメンの音楽隊（5） 37

animal	動物	lastly	最後に
at last	ついに、やっと	manage to	どうにかして〜する
back	背中	perch	止まる
be to	〜することになっている	place oneself	身を置く
climb upon	〜に登る	plan	計画
counsel　take counsel	話し合う	sit at a table	食事の席に着く
covered with	〜でおおわれた	sort	種類、タイプ
drink	飲む	table	テーブル、食卓
drive away	追い払う	then	すると、それから
eat	食べる	thing	こと、ものごと
enjoy oneself	楽しむ	think of	〜を思いつく
fly up	飛び上がる	together	いっしょに、みんなで
fore-feet	前足	upon	〜の上に
grey-horse	あし毛の馬	window-ledge	窓の下枠
head	頭	wish	〜だったらいいのになあ
jump on	〜に飛び乗る		

　ロバ、猟犬、ネコ、雄鶏が、今まさに泥棒たちを驚かそうとしている絵を描いてみましょう。絵が苦手な人は、ブレーメンという街がどこにあるか、インターネットで検索してみましょう。うまくいけば、動物たちが重なりあっている像の写真が載っている、観光案内のページにたどり着きます。ブレーメンがどんな街か、記録しておきましょう。（ブレーメンと言えば、サッカーファンなら、あの奥寺選手が所属したチームがあることはご存知のはず）

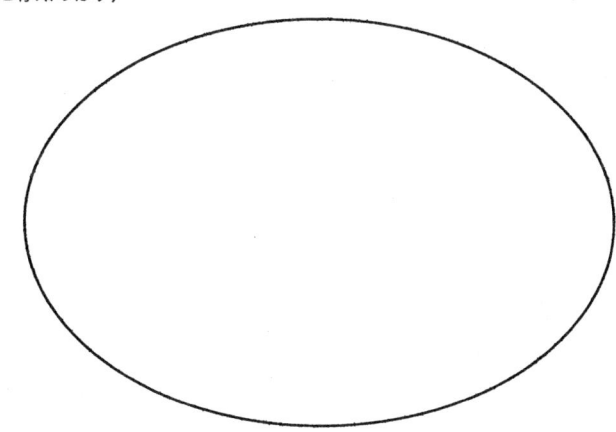

When this was done, at a given signal, they began to perform their music together: the donkey brayed, the hound barked, the cat mewed, and the cock crowed; then they burst through the window into the room, so that the glass clattered! At this horrible din, the robbers sprang up, thinking no otherwise than that a ghost had come in, and fled in a great fright out into the forest. The four companions now sat down at the table, well content with what was left, and ate as if they were going to fast for a month.

As soon as the four minstrels had done, they put out the light, and each sought for himself a sleeping-place according to his nature and to what suited him. The donkey laid himself down upon some straw in the yard, the hound behind the door, the cat upon the hearth near the warm ashes, and the cock perched himself upon a beam of the roof; and being tired from their long walk, they soon went to sleep.

準備ができると、あらかじめ決められた合図で、みんなが音楽を奏で始めました。ロバがいななき、猟犬が吠え、ネコがミャーオ、雄鶏がコケコッコー、と鳴きました。次に、彼らは窓から部屋の中へと押し入り、ガラスがガチャガチャと音をたてました。この恐ろしい物音を耳にすると、泥棒たちは飛び上がり、幽霊がやってきたに違いないと思い込み、森の中へと大変に肝をつぶして逃げ込みました。さて今度は、4匹の仲間たちが食卓につき、残り物でも大満足で、これから1か月は断食するのじゃないかというくらい食べました。

4楽人たちは食事を済ますと、早速火を消し、それぞれ自分の性質や好みに応じて寝場所を探しました。ロバは庭にいくらかあったわらの上に体を横たえ、猟犬は扉の内側に、ネコは暖かい灰のそばの炉辺の前に、そして雄鶏は屋根の梁の上に止まりました。そして長いこと歩いて疲れていたので、みんなはすぐに眠りにつきました。

ブレーメンの音楽隊（6） 39

according to	〜にしたがって	left	<leave 残す
as if	まるで〜のように	long	長い
as soon as	〜するとすぐに	mew	（猫が）ニャーと鳴く
ash	灰	minstrel	音楽家、楽人
at a given signal	決められた合図で	nature	性質、本性
ate	<eat 食べる	near	〜の近くで
bark	（犬が）吠える	no otherwise than	まさに
beam	梁（はり）	perch himself	止まる
behind	〜の後ろに	perform	演奏する
bray	（ロバが）いななく	roof	屋根
burst through	〜から突入する	sat	<sit
clatter	ガチャガチャ音を立てる	put out	消す
content with	〜に満足で	signal	合図、信号
din	やかましい音	sit down at the table	食卓につく
done	<do	sleeping place	寝場所、寝床
each	それぞれ	sought	<seek 探す
fast	断食する	sprang	<spring up 飛び上がる
fled	flee 逃げる	straw	わら
for a month	1か月間	suit	〜に合う、気に入る
for himself	自分で、一人で	tired from	〜して疲れて
fright	恐怖、恐れ	together	いっしょに、みんなで
ghost	幽霊、お化け	upon	〜の上に
given	あらかじめ決められた	walk	歩くこと、歩行
glass	ガラス	warm	暖かい
great	大変な、恐ろしい	well	すっかり、とても
hearth	炉辺、暖炉の前	window	窓
horrible	恐ろしい	yard	庭

then they burst through the window into the room, so that the glass clattered
それから、彼らは窓から部屋の中へと突入し、その結果ガラスがカタカタと音をたてた
thinking no otherwise than that a ghost had come in
　　　幽霊が入ってきたに違いないと思って
well content with (what was left)　（残されたところのもの）にとても満足して
being tired = as they were tired

When it was past midnight, and the robbers saw from afar that the light was no longer burning in their house, and all appeared quiet, the captain said, "We ought not to have let ourselves be frightened out of our wits;" and ordered one of them to go and examine the house.

The messenger finding all still, went into the kitchen to light a candle, and, taking the glistening fiery eyes of the cat for live coals, he held a lucifer-match to them to light it. But the cat did not understand the joke, and flew in his face, spitting and scratching. He was dreadfully frightened, and ran to the back-door, but the dog, who lay there, sprang up and bit his leg; and as he ran across the yard by the straw-heap, the donkey gave him a smart kick with its hind foot. The cock, too, who had been awakened by the noise, and had become lively, cried down from the beam, "Cock-a-doodle-doo!"

真夜中を過ぎ、泥棒たちは、もう火は燃えておらず、辺りも静かそうだ、と遠くから見て取ると、親分が言いました。「驚かされて正気を失ってはなんねえ」と。そして、1人に家を調べてくるように命じました。

使いの手下は辺りが静かなのを見ると、ロウソクに灯をともすために台所に入り、きらきらと燃え盛るようなネコの目を、燃えている石炭だと勘違いし、火をつけようとして黄リンマッチをネコの目に押し付けました。しかし、ネコはこのジョークを理解せず、手下の顔に飛びかかり、つばを吐きかけ、引っ掻き回しました。手下は恐怖のあまり恐れおののき、裏口へと走りましたが、今度はそこに寝ていた犬が飛び上がり、手下の足に噛み付きました。庭を横切ってわらの山のわきを走って行くと、ロバが後ろ足で彼に強烈な一撃をお見舞いしました。雄鶏も騒ぎで目を覚まし、興奮して、梁の上から「コケコッコー」と叫びました。

across	〜を横切って	kitchen	台所	
afar	遠く from afar 遠くから	lay	<lie いる、横たわる	
appear	〜と思われる、見える	leg	足	
awaken	起こす、目覚めさせる	let	〜させる	
back-door	裏口	light	明かり；火をつける	
bit	<bite 噛む	live	燃え盛る	
candle	ロウソク	lively	元気な	
captain	親分、首領、お頭	lucifer-match	黄リンマッチ	
coal	石炭	messenger	使い、手下	
cock-a-doodle-doo	コケコッコー	midnight	真夜中	
cry	鳴く	no longer	もう〜でない	
dreadfully	恐ろしく、とても	noise	騒音、騒ぎ	
examine	調べる	order	命ずる、命令する	
eye	目	ought to	〜すべきである	
face	顔	past	〜を過ぎて	
find	見つける、分かる	quiet	静かな、落ち着いた	
fiery	火のように赤い	scratch	引っかく	
flew	<fly 飛ぶ	smart	きつい、効く	
foot	脚	spit	つばを吐く	
frighten	驚かせる	still	静かな、シンとした	
glistening	キラキラ光る	straw-heap	わらの山	
held	hold 持つ、差し出す	take ... for	...を〜と思う	
hind	後ろの hind foot 後ろ足	too	も、また	
joke	冗談、悪ふざけ	wits	正気、平静さ	
kick	蹴り	out of one's wits 取り乱して		

all appeared quiet すべてが静かに見えた
we ought not to have let ourselves be frightened out of our wits
驚かされて取り乱すことを私たち自身にさせるべきではなかった
the messenger finding all still, went into the kitchen
使いの者は静かと分かると台所へ入った
taking the glistening fiery eyes of the cat for live coals
火のようにキラキラ光るネコの目を燃え盛る石炭だと思って
he held a lucifer-match to them to light it
彼は差し出した、黄リンマッチを、それら（目）に、火をつけるために
the dog, who lay there, sprang up and bit his leg
猟犬は（そこに横になっていたのだが）飛び上がって彼の足を噛んだ

Then the robber ran back as fast as he could to his captain, and said, "Ah, there is a horrible witch sitting in the house, who spat on me and scratched my face with her long claws; and by the door stands a man with a knife, who stabbed me in the leg; and in the yard there lies a black monster, who beat me with a wooden club; and above, upon the roof, sits the judge, who called out, 'Bring the rogue here to me!' so I got away as well as I could."

After this the robbers did not trust themselves in the house again; but it suited the four musicians of Bremen so well that they did not care to leave it any more. And the mouth of him who last told this story is still warm.

するとその泥棒は親分のところへ全速力でもどって、言いました。「あのう、家の中には恐ろしい魔女が陣取っとります。つばを吐きかけられて、長い爪で顔を引っ掻かれっちまいました。ドアんとこには刃物を持った男が立ってて、足を刺されちまいました。庭には黒い怪物がいて、こん棒で殴られっちまいました。そんでもって、高いとこ、屋根の上には裁判官様が座ってやす。そのお方は『ごろつきどもをここ、私のところへ連れて来い』って大声で叫んどりましたです。ですんで、なんとか、かんとか、逃げ出して来たってわけっす」

この後、泥棒たちが安心してその家にやって来る、ということは二度とありませんでした。ですが、その家はブレーメンの４人の音楽家たちにとってはおあつらえ向きだったので、もうそこからよそへ行こうとは思いませんでした。そうして、最後にこの話をした人の唇はまだ温かいのです。

above	上方に、上の方に	monster	怪物
again	再び、また	mouth	口
ah	えーと、あのー	musician	音楽家
as fast as he could	全速力で	not ... any more	もう〜でない
as well as I could	なんとか	rogue	ごろつき、悪者
back	もどって	spat	<spit つばを吐く
beat	たたく、打つ	stab	刺す
black	黒い	stand	立っている、いる
bring	連れて来る	still	まだ
by	〜の所、傍ら	story	話
call out	叫ぶ、大声を出す	suit	合う、気に入る
care	not care to 〜がいやと思う	told	<tell 話す、語る
claw	つめ	trust	安心して〜する
club	こん棒	trust themselves in the house	安心してその家にいる
got	<get away 逃げ出す	upon	〜の上に
horrible	恐ろしい、ひどい	warm	温かい
judge	裁判官、判事	well	よく
knife	ナイフ	witch	魔女
last	最後に、一番最近	wooden	木の、木製の
leave	去る、出て行く		
lie	いる、横たわる		

then the robber ran back as fast as he could
　　　　それから、その泥棒はできるだけ早く走ってもどった
there is a horrible witch sitting in the house, who spat on me and scratched my face　おそろしい魔女が家の中に座っていて、
　　　　そしてそいつが私につばをかけ、顔を引っ掻いた
by the door stands a man with a knife, who stabbed me in the leg
　　　　ドアのところにはナイフを持った男がいて、そいつが私の足を刺した

it suited the four musicians of Bremen so well that they did not care to leave it
それ（家）はブレーメンの4楽人にとてもよくあった。その結果彼らは家を出る気にはならなかった

And the mouth of him who last told this story is still warm
彼（←この話を最後に[つまり一番最近]した人）の口はまだ温かい
　　　　つまり、この話はそんなに昔のものではない

Cinderella; or the Little Glass Slipper

Once there was a gentleman who married for his second wife the proudest and most haughty woman that was ever seen. She had by a former husband two daughters of her own humor, who were, indeed, exactly like her in all things. He had likewise, by another wife, a young daughter, but of unparalleled goodness and sweetness of temper, which she took from her mother, who was the best creature in the world.

No sooner were the ceremonies of the wedding over but the mother-in-law began to show herself in her true colors. She could not bear the good qualities of this pretty girl, and the less because they made her own daughters appear the more odious. She employed her in meanest work of the house: she scoured the dishes, tables, etc., and scrubbed madam's chamber and those of misses, her daughters; she lay up in a sorry garret, upon a wretched straw bed, while her sisters lay in fine rooms, with floors all inlaid, upon beds of the very newest fashion, and where they had looking-glasses so large that they might see themselves at their full length from head to foot.

シンデレラ、あるいは小さなガラスの靴

　むかし、ある立派な男が、２番目の奥さんとして、最も気位が高く最も高慢な女性を迎えました。奥方には、前夫との間に自分の性格にそっくりな２人の娘があり、その娘たちは本当に何をやるにも母親に瓜二つでした。同じく夫の方にも前妻との間に幼い娘がおりましたが、こちらは比類なき善性を備え、優しい性格で、娘は自分の母親からそれらを受け継いでおり、その母親はこの世で一番すてきな人だったのでした。
　結婚の儀式が済むと、すぐに継母は正体を現し始めました。彼女はこのかわいい子供のよい性質に我慢ができませんでした。自分の娘がいっそう憎らしく見えるのですから、なおさらのことでした。継母は彼女を家の中で一番汚らしい仕事に使いました。皿やテーブルなどを磨いたり、そして奥様の部屋や、奥様の娘であるお嬢様たちの部屋を磨き上げました。その子はみじめな屋根裏部屋で、見るも無惨なわらのベッドに寝ました。その一方で、お姉さんたちはピカピカに床を張ったすてきな部屋で、最新式のベッドに休みました。そしてお姉さんたちの部屋には大きな姿見があり、それは頭のてっぺんからつま先まで全身が映るとても大きなものでした。

all	すべての；すっかり	less	より少ない
another	もうひとりの、別の	like	〜のような
appear	見える	likewise	同じように、同様に
bear	耐える、我慢する	looking-glass	鏡、姿見
best	一番よい	madam	奥様、奥方
by	〜によって、との間に	married	<marry 結婚する
ceremonies	<ceremony 儀式	mean	みすぼらしい、粗末な
chamber	部屋、寝室	miss	お嬢様
color	in her true colors ありのままの姿で	mother-in-law	継母
		odious	不愉快な、憎らしい
creature	生き物、人	once	かつて、むかし
daughter	娘	over	終わって、済んで
dish	皿、食器	own	自身の、自分の
employ	使う、使用する	proudest	<proud 高慢な
etc.	などなど	qualities	<quality 性質
ever	これまで、かつて	scour	磨く
exactly	まったく、すっかり	scrub	磨き上げる
fashion	流行、はやり	sooner	no sooner 〜するとすぐに
floor	床	sorry	気の毒な、かわいそうな
for	〜として	straw	わら
former	以前の、かつての	sweetness	優しさ
from 〜 to	〜から...まで	temper	性格
full	完全な、十分な	take	受け継ぐ
garret	屋根裏部屋	true	真の、本当の
gentleman	紳士、殿方	unparalleled	比類なき、最高の
goodness	よいこと、善、優しさ	upon	〜の上に
haughty	傲慢な、横柄な	very	とても
humor	性質、性格、気質	wedding	結婚、婚礼
husband	夫	while	〜の一方
in	〜の中で、において	wife	奥さん、配偶者
indeed	実に、実際に	with	〜した、をともなった
inlaid	敷きつめられた	work	仕事
large	大きな	world	世の中
lay	<lie up 休む、横になる	wretched	あわれな、粗末な
length	長さ		

Cinderella(2)

The poor girl bore all patiently and dared not tell her father, who would have rattled her off; for his wife governed him entirely. When she had done her work she used to go into the chimney-corner and sit down among cinders and ashes, which made her commonly be called a cinder maid; but the youngest, who was not so rude and uncivil as the eldest, called her Cinderella. However, Cinderella, notwithstanding her mean apparel, was a hundred times handsomer than her sisters, though they were always dressed very richly.

It happened that the King's son gave a ball and invited all persons, of fashion to it. Our young misses were also invited, for they cut a very grand figure among the quality. They were mightily delighted at this invitation, and wonderfully busy in choosing out such gowns, petticoats, and head-clothes as might become them. This was a new trouble to Cinderella, for it was she who ironed her sisters' linen and plaited their ruffles. They talked all day long of nothing but how they should be dressed.

"For my part," said the eldest, "I will wear my red velvet suit with French trimming."

　かわいそうな少女は何事にもよく耐え、自分の父親には言おうとはしませんでした。父親はおそらく何のかんのといって、彼女をたしなめたでしょう。なぜなら、奥様の尻にしっかりと敷かれていたからです。その子は、仕事を終えると部屋の隅にある、暖炉の煙突のところへ行き、消し炭や灰に囲まれて座っていたものでした。このため、消し炭娘とよく呼ばれていました。でも、妹の方は姉ほどは失礼でも無作法でもなかったので、その子のことをシンデレラ（消し炭お嬢さん）と呼びました。しかし、シンデレラはみすぼらしい服にもかかわらず、姉たちの100倍もきれいでした。いつも姉たちはとても豪華に着飾っていたにもかかわらずです。
　王様のご子息が舞踏会を開催されることになり、みなを招待しました。貴族の人たちみなを舞踏会に。私たちのお嬢さんたちもまた招かれました。なぜなら、上流階級の中でも、特に羽振りがよかったからでした。お嬢様たちはこの招待に大喜びし、自分に似合うようなドレスや、下着や、髪飾りを選ぶのに、たいへん大忙しでした。これはシンデレラにとっては、新しい悩みの種でした。なぜなら、お姉様方の下着にアイロンをかけ、ひだのついた飾りを整えるのは、みなシンデレラの仕事だったからです。お姉様方は、一日中、何を着ていこうかしら、とばかり話していました。
　「私はね」と姉が言いました。「フランス風の縁取りがついた、ビロードのおそろいを着ていくことにするわ」

all day long	一日中	invitation	招待
among	～の中で、間で	invite	招待する
apparel	服、衣服	iron	アイロンをかける
ashes	灰	king	王様
ball	舞踏会、ダンスパーティー	linen	下着
become	似合う、ふさわしい	made	\<make ～させる
bore	\<bear 耐える、我慢する	maid	少女、乙女
busy in	～に忙しい	mightily	非常に、ものすごく
call	呼ぶ	nothing but	～のことばかり
chimney-corner	煙突がある部屋の隅	notwithstanding	～にもかかわらず
choose out	選び出す	part	for my part 自分としては
cinder	消し炭	patiently	辛抱強く
Cinderella	消し炭＋お嬢様	petticoat	女性用の服、ドレス
commonly	普通は、下品に	plait	編む
cut a figure	印象を与える	poor	かわいそうな、気の毒な
dare	あえて～する	quality	上流階級
(be) delighted at	～を喜ぶ	rattle off	(早口で) まくしたてる
(be) dressed richly	豪勢に装う	richly	豪華に、ぜいたくに
eldest	一番年上の	rude	無作法な、無教養の
entirely	すっかり、完全に	ruffle	ひだ飾り
(of)fashion	上流階級の	son	息子、(男の) 子供
for	～なので	such ... as	～のような
French	フランスの、フランス風の	suit	スーツ、そろいの服
gave	\<give a ball 舞踏会を催す	though	～ではあるが
govern	支配する、治める	times	回、回数
gown	(女性正装用の) ドレス	trimming	縁取り、ふち飾り
grand	立派な	trouble	問題、困難
handsome	見栄えのする、立派な	uncivil	無作法な、無礼な
happen	起こる	used to	よく～したものだった
head-cloth	髪に飾る布	velvet	ビロードの
however	しかし	wear	着る、身に付ける
hundred	100、百	wonderfully	とても

"And I," said the youngest, "shall have my usual petticoat; but then, to make amends for that, I will put on my gold-flowered manteau and my diamond stomacher, which is far from being the most ordinary one in the world."

They sent for the best tire-woman they could get to make up their headdresses and adjust their double pinners, and they had their red brushes and patches from Mademoiselle de la Poche.

Cinderella was likewise called up to them to be consulted in all these matters, for she had excellent notions and advised them always for the best, nay, and offered her services to dress their heads, which they were very willing she should do. As she was doing this they said to her:

"Cinderella, would you not be glad to go to the ball?"

"Alas!" said she, "you only jeer me. It is not for such as I am to go thither."

"Thou art in the right of it," replied they. "It would make the people laugh to see a cinder wench at a ball."

「それじゃ私は」と妹が言いました、「いつものドレスにするわ。でも、それじゃつまらないから、金の花柄のマントと、ダイヤのついた胸飾りにするわ。そうすればとっても在り来たりっていうわけではなくなるわね」

お嬢様方は、髪飾りを作り、ダブルピンナーを合わせるために、最高の仕立て屋を呼び寄せ、赤い房と当て布を、デ・ラ・ポッシュ嬢の店から取り寄せました。

シンデレラは、いつもと同じように、こういったことの相談を持ちかけられるために、呼びつけられました。なぜならシンデレラは、こういったことをよく承知しており、いつも最高の助言をしたからでした。いえいえ、それだけでなく、髪を整える手伝いを申し出たりもしました。シンデレラがそうすることは、大歓迎されました。シンデレラがそうしていると、姉妹が彼女に言いました。

「シンデレラ、あんたも舞踏会に行きたいのじゃなくって」

「とんでもありません」と彼女は言いました、「私をおからかいになって。そこは私のようなものが行くところではありませんわ」

「あんたの言う通りね」と姉妹は答えました、「舞踏会で消し炭っ子を見たら、みんな笑っちゃうわね」

adjust	合わせる、調節する	make amends	埋め合わせをする
advise	助言する	make up	あつらえる
alas	ああ、悲しいことに	make ... laugh	笑わせる
always	いつも	manteau	マント
amends	償い、埋め合わせ	matter	こと、物事
brush	ふさ、ふさ飾り	nay	それどころか
call up	呼びつける	notion	意見、考え
cinder	消し炭、燃え殻、灰	offer	申し出る
consult	相談する	ordinary	普通の
diamond	ダイヤモンド	patch	当て布
double	二重の	pinner	（垂れをピンでとめた）帽子
dress	飾る、整える	put on	着る、身につける
excellent	すばらしい、すてきな	replied	<reply 返事をする
far from	〜からほど遠い	right in the right	正しい
get	手に入れる	send for	呼びにやる
glad	うれしい	services	奉仕、手伝い、世話
gold-flowered	金で花の模様をいれた	stomacher	胸飾り
headdress	髪飾り	thither	そこへ
head	頭（髪）	thou art	= you are
jeer	からかう、ひやかす	tire-woman	仕立屋
laugh	笑う	usual	いつもの、普通の
Mademoiselle de la Poche	デ・ラ・ポッシュ嬢（の店）	wench	娘っ子
		willing	〜を望んでいる

シンデレラ（3） 49

Any one but Cinderella would have dressed their heads awry, but she was very good and dressed them perfectly well. They were almost two days without eating, so much they were transported with joy. They broke above a dozen of laces in trying to be laced up close, that they might have a fine, slender shape, and they were continually at their looking-glass. At last the happy day came. They went to Court, and Cinderella followed them with her eyes as long as she could, and when she had lost sight of them she fell a-crying.

Her Godmother, who saw her all in tears, asked her what was the matter.

"I wish I could--I wish I could--"

She was not able to speak the rest being interrupted by her tears and sobbing.

This Godmother of hers, who was a fairy, said to her: "Thou wishest thou could'st go to the ball. Is it not so?"

"Y--es," cried Cinderella, with a great sigh.

"Well," said her Godmother, "be but a good girl, and I will contrive that thou shalt go." Then she took her into her chamber and said to her: "Run into the garden and bring me a pumpkin."

シンデレラを除いて、だれがやっても髪はきちんとは整えられなかったでしょうが、彼女はとても上手に、完璧に飾り終えました。姉妹はほとんど２日間食事を取っていませんでした。それほどうれしくて、夢中だったのです。姉妹は、ぴっちりと胴回りを締め上げてもらうために１ダース以上のひもを切ってしまいました。見栄えがよく、やせて見えるようにするためです。そうして彼女たちは始終姿見の前に立っていました。ついに、その悦ばしい日が来ました。姉妹は宮廷へ出かけ、シンデレラは目が届く限り、お姉さんたちを目で追いましたが、姿が見えなくなると、どっと泣き出しました。

シンデレラの教母様は、彼女が涙に暮れているのを見ると、どうしたのかと尋ねました。

「…できたらいいのに、…できたらいいのに」

シンデレラは、涙とむせび泣きにさえぎられて、全部言うことができません。

このシンデレラの教母様は、実は妖精だったのですけれども、彼女に言いました。

「舞踏会に行きたいのでしょう。そうじゃなくって」

「ふぁーぁい」とシンデレラは大声を出し、大きなため息をつきました。

「ようござんしょう」と教母様が言いました、「本当によい子におし。そうすればお前が行けるようにしてあげましょう」それから教母様はシンデレラを彼女の部屋へ連れて行き、言いました。

「庭の畑へ走ってお行き。そしてカボチャを取ってきてちょうだい」

シンデレラ（4）

above	〜より多く	into	〜の中へ
all	すっかり、まったく	joy	喜び、うれしさ
almost	ほとんど	lace up	（ひもなどで）締め上げる
any	どんな	lace	（コルセットの）ひも
as long as	〜の限りは	looking-glass	鏡、姿見
ask	尋ねる	lost	<lose sight of 見失う
at last	ついに、やっと	matter	困難、困ったこと
awry	曲がった、ゆがんで	one	ひと
be able to	〜できる	perfectly	完全に、完璧に
bring	持って来る	pumpkin	カボチャ
broke	<break 切る、壊す	rest	残り
but	〜を除いて；本当に	saw	<see 見る
chamber	部屋、寝室	shalt....	thou shalt = you shall
close	ぴったりと、きつく	shape	姿、体形
continually	いつも、絶えず	sigh	ため息
contrive	工夫する、うまくやる	sight	ながめ、視界
court	（王様の）宮廷、王宮	slender	細い、すらりとした
cry	泣く、大声を出す	sobbing	しゃくり上げ、むせび泣き
dozen	1ダース、12個	speak	話す、言葉にする
dress	着せる、着付ける	tear	涙
fairy	妖精	thou = you	
fell a-crying	<fall a-crying 泣き出す	took	<take 連れて行く
follow	追う、追いかける	transported	うっとりする、舞上がる
garden	庭、庭の畑、菜園	try to	〜しようと努力する
godmother	名付け親、教母	well	上手に；ええと、さて
head	頭、頭髪	wish	願う、望む
in tears	涙を流して	thou wishest = you wish	
interrupt	邪魔をする、さえぎる	without	〜なしで

Cinderella went immediately to gather the finest she could get and brought it to her Godmother, not being able to imagine how this pumpkin could make her go to the ball. Her Godmother scooped out all the inside of it, having left nothing but the rind; which done, she struck it with her wand, and the pumpkin was instantly turned into a fine coach, gilded all over with gold.

She then went to look into her mousetrap, where she found six mice all alive, and ordered Cinderella to lift up a little the trapdoor, when, giving each mouse as it went out a little tap with her wand, the mouse was that moment turned into a fine horse, which altogether made a very fine set of six horses of a beautiful mouse-colored dapple-gray. Being at a loss for a coachman, Cinderella said:

"I will go and see if there is never a rat in the rattrap--we may make a coachman of him."

"Thou art in the right," replied her Godmother. "Go and look."

Cinderella brought the trap to her, and in it there were three huge rats. The fairy made choice of one of the three which had the largest beard, and having touched him with her wand he was turned into a fat, jolly coachman, who had the smartest whiskers eyes ever beheld. After that she said to her:

シンデレラはすぐに一番よいものを取りに行き、教母様のところへ持って来ましたが、このカボチャが一体どうやって舞踏会へ連れて行ってくれるのか想像することができませんでした。教母様は、カボチャの中身をみんな掻き出し、皮だけを残しました。それが終ると、教母様はカボチャをつえで打ちました。するとカボチャは瞬時に金色に塗られたすばらしい馬車に変わりました。

教母様はそれから、ねずみ捕りをのぞきに行き、その中に生きた6匹のねずみを見つけると、シンデレラにねずみ捕りの入り口を少し持ち上げるように命じ、ねずみが出てくる時に、それぞれにつえで軽く触れると、ねずみはすばらしい馬に変わり、ねずみ色に黒のぶちの6頭立てができました。馬車の御者がいないことに気付くと、シンデレラは言いました。「どぶねずみ捕りに、どぶねずみが入ってないか行って見て来ます。それで御者ができますわ」「言う通りね」教母様が答えました、「行って見てらっしゃい」

シンデレラがねずみ捕りを持って来ると、中にはとても大きなどぶねずみが3匹いました。妖精は3匹の中からあごひげが一番長い1匹を選び、つえで触れるとそれは太っちょで陽気な御者になり、見たこともないほどすてきなほおひげを蓄えていました。それから妖精はシンデレラに言いました。

シンデレラ（5）

a little	少し	lift up	持ち上げる
alive	生きている、生きたまま	look into	～の中をのぞく
all over	辺り一面、全部	loss	at a loss for ～がない
altogether	合わせて、全部で	made	<make ～になる；～にする
at a loss for	～に困って	make choice of	～を選ぶ
beard	あごひげ	mice	<mouse ねずみ
beautiful	すてきな、すばらしい	moment	瞬間
beheld	<behold 見る、見つめる	mouse-colored	ねずみ色の
brought	<bring	mousetrap	ねずみ捕り
choice	選択	nothing but	～だけ
coach	馬車	order	命令する
coachman	御者、馬車の運転手	rat	どぶねずみ、大ねずみ
dapple-gray	ねずみ色に黒のぶちの	rattrap	大ねずみ捕り
each	それぞれの	replied	<reply 答える、返事をする
ever	それまでに、かつて	right	in the right 正しい
fat	太った、でぶの	rind	皮、外皮
finest	一番すばらしい	scoop	掻き出す、すくい出す
found	<find 見つける	see if	～かどうか見る
gather	収穫する、取り入れる	set	ひとそろいの
gilded	金メッキした	smart	洗練された
gold	金	struck	<strike 打つ、たたく
huge	大きな、巨大な	tap	軽く触れる
imagine	想像する、思い描く	touch	触れる、触る
immediately	すぐに、即座に	trap	わな
inside	内側、内部	trapdoor	わなの入り口
instantly	すぐに、その場で	turn into	～になる
jolly	陽気な、楽しい	wand	つえ
largest	<large 大きい	went	<go out 外に出る
left	<leave 残す	whiskers	ほおひげ

"Go again into the garden, and you will find six lizards behind the watering-pot. Bring them to me."

She had no sooner done so but her Godmother turned them into six footmen, who skipped up immediately behind the coach, with their liveries all bedaubed with gold and silver, and clung as close behind each other as if they had done nothing else their whole lives. The fairy then said to Cinderella:

"Well, you see here an equipage fit to go to the ball with. Are you not pleased with it?"

"Oh! yes," cried she; "but must I go thither as I am, in these dirty rags?"

Her Godmother only just touched her with her wand, and at the same instant her clothes were turned into cloth-of-gold and silver, all beset with jewels. Ah! who can describe a robe made by the fairies? It was white as snow, and as dazzling; round the hem hung a fringe of diamonds, sparkling like dewdrops in the sunshine. The lace about the throat and arms could only have been spun by fairy spiders. Surely it was a dream! Cinderella put her daintily gloved hand to her throat, and softly touched the pearls that encircled her neck.

「もう一度菜園へ行きなさい、そうすると水がめの後ろに、とかげが6匹見つかるでしょう。捕って来てちょうだい」

シンデレラがそうすると、すぐに教母様はとかげを6人の従僕に変えました。すると従僕たちは、金や銀で飾り立てたそろいの制服を着てすぐに急いで馬車の後ろに整列し、生涯ほかに何もしたことがないかのように、お互いがぴったりとくっついて並びました。その妖精はそれからシンデレラに言いました。「さて、舞踏会に行くのにふさわしい馬車と供まわりの準備ができたわねえ。うれしくはないかい」「ええ、うれしいです」とシンデレラが叫びました、「でもこのままそこへ行かなければ行けないんですか、この薄汚いぼろを着たままで」

教母様はシンデレラにつえでちょっと触れただけでしたが、その同じ瞬間に彼女の服は金糸銀糸の衣装に変わり、あちらこちらに宝石がちりばめられていました。そうです、一体だれが妖精の作った優雅な服を言葉で言い表すことができましょうか。それは雪のように白く、目もくらみそうでした。へりに沿ってダイヤの房飾りがぶら下がり、まるで朝日に照らされた霧のしずくのように光り輝いています。首や腕回りのレースは、妖精の国のクモだけが紡ぐことができるようなものでした。確かにそれは夢のようでした。シンデレラが可憐な手袋をはめた手をのど元においてみると、首の回りにかかった真珠の首飾りに手が触れました。

シンデレラ（6） 55

about	〜のまわり	just	ちょっと
again	もう一度、また	lace	レース
ah	ああ、なるほど、やっぱり	like	〜のように
all	全面に、すっかり	liveries	<livery お仕着せ、制服
arm	腕	lives	<life 人生
as I am	このままの姿で	lizard	とかげ
as if	まるで〜のように	neck	首
bedaub	塗り立てる、飾り立てる	nothing else	ほかに何もない
behind	〜の後ろに	oh	おお、おや、ああ
beset with	〜で飾られた	only	〜だけ、ほんの〜
close	ぴったりと、接近して	pearl	真珠　pearls 真珠の首飾り
cloth-of gold and silver	金糸銀糸の布	pleased with	〜でうれしい
		put	置く、当てる
clothes	服	rags	ぼろ切れ、みすぼらしい服
clung	<cling ぴったりと並ぶ	robe	優雅な服
daintily	優雅に、かれんに	round	〜の回りに
dazzling	目もくらむほどの	same	同じ
describe	描写する、言い表す	skip	跳ね飛ぶように急いで行く
dewdrop	霧のしずく	snow	雪
diamond	ダイヤモンド	softly	やさしく、そっと
dirty	汚い、薄汚れた	sooner	had no sooner 〜 but ... 〜するとすぐに ...
dream	夢		
each other	お互い、それぞれ	sparkle	輝く
encircle	〜の周りを取り囲む	spider	クモ
equipage	馬車と供まわり	spun	<spin 紡いで〜にする
fairies	<fairy 妖精	sunshine	太陽の光
fit	ふさわしい、適切な	surely	確かに
footman	従僕、下僕	thither	そこへ
fringe	ふさ飾り	throat	のど、首回り
gloved	手袋をした	touch	触る、触れる
hand	手	turn 〜 into	〜を...にする
hem	へり、ふち	watering-pot	水がめ
hung	<hang 下がる、掛かる	white	白い
instant	瞬間	whole	すべての、全
jewel	宝石		

"Come, child," said the Godmother, "or you will be late."

As Cinderella moved, the firelight shone upon her dainty shoes.

"They are of diamonds," she said.

"No," answered her Godmother, smiling; "they are better than that--they are of glass, made by the fairies. And now, child, go, and enjoy yourself to your heart's content."

But her Godmother, above all things, commanded her not to stay till after midnight, telling her at the same time that if she stayed one moment longer the coach would be a pumpkin again, her horses mice, her coachman a rat, her footmen lizards, and her clothes become just as they were before.

「いらっしゃい、お前」教母様が言いました、「さもないと遅れますよ」
シンデレラが身を動かすと、暖炉の火の明かりが優美な靴に映えました。
「ダイヤモンドでできているのね」シンデレラが言いました。
「いいえ」と教母様が微笑みながら答えました、「それよりももっといいものよ。ガラス製なの。妖精たちが作ったガラスなのよ。さあ、お前、行きなさい。そして心ゆくまで楽しんでらっしゃい」
ですが、教母様は、とりわけ真夜中よりも遅くまでいないように、と命令しました。そして同時に次のように言いました。一瞬でも長くいたら、馬車はまたカボチャに、馬はねずみに、御者はどぶねずみに、従僕はとかげに、服は前と同じように、もどってしまうと。

above all things	とりわけ、なかでも	glass	ガラス
answer	答える、返事をする	late	遅れて
as	〜につれて、すると	longer	より長く
at the same time	同時に	midnight	真夜中
become	〜になる	moment	瞬間、一瞬
better than	〜よりよい	move	動く
command	命令する、命ずる	now	さて、さあ
content	満足	of	〜製の、でできている
to your heart's content	心ゆくまで	or	さもないと、そうでないと
dainty	上品な、すてきな	shoes	靴
enjoy yourself	楽しむ	shone	<shine upon 〜に反射する
firelight	(暖炉の) 火明かり	smiling	微笑みながら
		stay	とどまっている、滞在する
		till after midnight	真夜中過ぎまで

She promised her Godmother she would not fail of leaving the ball before midnight, and then away she drives, scarce able to contain herself for joy. The King's son, who was told that a great Princess, whom nobody knew, was come, ran out to receive her. He gave her his hand as she alighted out of the coach; and led her into the hall among all the company. There was immediately a profound silence, they left off dancing, and the violins ceased to play, so attentive was every one to contemplate the singular beauties of the unknown newcomer. Nothing was then heard but a confused noise of "Ha! how handsome she is! Ha! how handsome she is!"

The King himself, old as he was, could not help watching her and telling the Queen softly that it was a long time since he had seen so beautiful and lovely a creature.

All the ladies were busied in considering her clothes and headdress, that they might have some made next day after the same pattern, provided they could meet with such fine materials and as able hands to make them.

シンデレラは、必ず真夜中前に舞踏会を退席する、と教母様に誓うと、それから馬車で出かけて行きましたが、うれしくてほとんどじっとしてはいられませんでした。王様のご子息は、だれも知らない、すてきなお姫様がやって来たと告げられると、出迎えに走りました。彼はシンデレラが馬車を降りるのに手を貸し、一同が集まっている中を、彼女の手を引いて広間まで案内しました。すぐに深い静寂が訪れ、みなが踊りをやめ、バイオリンの音がやみました。みなが見ず知らずの新参者の、まれに見る美しさに見とれて、気を取られてしまったのでした。それからは我を忘れた「ああ、なんてお美しい方なんでしょう。ああ、なんてお美しい方なんでしょう」というつぶやきしか聞こえてきませんでした。

王様自身も、年をとってはおりましたが、彼女を見つめずにはおられず、お妃に、こんなに美しい人を見るのは久しぶりだ、とそっとつぶやかずにはいられませんでした。

ご婦人方は、みなシンデレラの衣装や髪飾りの品定めに余念がありません。もし、そんなに上等な素材や、それらを作れる腕っこきの職人を探し出すことができれば、翌日に同じ形のものを多少なりとも作らせようとしていました。

able	〜できる；有能な	lovely	すてきな
after	〜をまねて、ならって	material	材料、原料
alight	降りる	meet with	（偶然）出会う
among	〜の中を	newcomer	新しく来た人、新参者
attentive to	〜に気を取られて	next day	次の日、翌日
beauties	美しい姿	nobody	だれも〜ない
be busied in	〜するのに忙しい	noise	騒音、物音
cease to	〜するのをやめる	old	年をとっている
company	集まった人々、来客	out of	〜から外へ
confused	混乱した、まごついた	pattern	型、形
consider	よく検討する	play	演奏する、音楽を奏でる
contain herself	自分を抑える	princess	お姫様
contemplate	じっと見つめる	profound	深い
could not help -ing	〜せずにいられなかった	promise	約束する
		provided	もし〜ならば
dance	踊る	queen	王妃
drive away	馬車で出かけて行く	ran	<run out 走り出る
fail of	〜しない、おこたる	receive	出迎える
for joy	喜びのために、うれしくて	scarce	ほとんど〜ない
ha	はあ、ほお、おや	silence	静寂、静けさ
hall	広間、大広間	since	〜以来
hand	手；職人の手、職人わざ	singular	並外れた、まれにみる
handsome	きれいな、すてきな	so	とても
have some made	いくつか作らせる	softly	やさしく、そっと
heard	<hear 聞く、耳にする	told	<tell 言う、告げる
knew	<know 知っている	unknown	知らない、見知らぬ
leaving	<leave 去る、退出する	violin	バイオリン
led	<lead into 〜へと導く	watch	見る、観察する
left	<leave off 〜をやめる		

The King's son conducted her to the most honorable seat and afterward took her out to dance with him. She danced so very gracefully that they all more and more admired her. A fine collation was served up, whereof the young Prince ate not a morsel, so intently was he busied in gazing on her.

She went and sat down by her sisters, showing them a thousand civilities, giving them part of the oranges and citrons which the Prince had presented her with, which very much surprised them, for they did not know her. While Cinderella was thus amusing her sisters, she heard the clock strike eleven and three-quarters, whereupon she immediately made a courtesy to the company and hastened away as fast as she could.

Being got home, she ran to seek out her Godmother, and after having thanked her she said she could not but heartily wish she might go next day to the ball, because the King's son had desired her.

As she was eagerly telling her Godmother what had passed at the ball her two sisters knocked at the door, which Cinderella ran and opened.

王様のご子息はシンデレラを一番よい席へ案内し、その後に自分と踊ってくださいと彼女をダンスへ連れ出しました。シンデレラは、それはそれは優雅に踊ったので、皆はよりいっそう彼女をほめそやしました。とてもおいしい軽食が出されましたが、若い王子はそれにはちっとも手を付けず、彼女を見つめることに夢中になっていました。

シンデレラは、お姉さんたちのところへ行き腰を下ろし、数えきれないほどの社交辞令を交わして、王子がシンデレラに進呈したオレンジやミカンを分けてあげたりしましたが、それはお姉様たちをとても驚かせました。なぜなら、お姉様たちは彼女がだれだか分からなかったからです。こうして、お姉様たちの目を白黒させているうちに、シンデレラは時計が１１時４５分を打つのを耳にしました。そうすると、彼女はすぐに皆さんに失礼のないように挨拶をし、全速力で帰り道を急ぎました。

シンデレラは家に帰り着くと、教母様を探して走り回り、教母様にお礼を言った後で、また明日も舞踏会に行きたいと心から願わないわけにはいかない、なぜなら王様のご子息が、彼女が来ることを望んでいるから、と言いました。

シンデレラが一生懸命に教母様に舞踏会での出来事を話していると、２人の姉妹が玄関をたたき、シンデレラはそこへと急ぎ、玄関を開けました。

admire	感心する、ほめる	more and more	よりいっそう
afterward	後に、後で	morsel	少量、ひとかけら
amuse	楽しませる、笑わせる	open	開ける、開く
as fast as she could	全速力で	orange	オレンジ
ate	<eat 食べる	part	部分、一部
by	～のそばに、傍らに	pass	過ぎる、起こる
citron	シトロン、みかん	present ... with	...に～を贈る
civility	丁寧な言葉	prince	王子
clock	時計	sat	<sit down 座る、腰を下ろす
collation	軽い食事	seat	椅子、席
conduct	導く、案内する	seek out	探し出す
could not but	～せずにはいられなかった	serve up	（食事などを）出す
		show	示す、見せる
courtesy	礼儀、丁寧な言葉遣い	strike	打つ
dance	踊る、ダンスする	surprise	驚かせる
desire	強く願う、求める	thank	感謝する
door	玄関	thousand	千の、たくさんの
eagerly	熱心に	three-quarters = 45分 (15×3)	
gaze	見つめる、まじまじと見る	thus	このようにして
gracefully	上品に、しとやかに	took	<take her out 彼女を連れ出す
hasten away	急いでその場を去る	whereof	それについて、そのうち
heartily	心から、熱心に	whereupon	その時、そこで
honorable	名誉ある、よい	while	～しているうちに
intently	熱心に、夢中になって	wish	願う、望む
knock at	～をノックする		

"How long you have stayed!" cried she, gaping, rubbing her eyes, and stretching herself as if she had been just waked out of her sleep. She had not, however, had any manner of inclination to sleep since they went from home.

"If thou hadst been at the ball," said one of her sisters, "thou would'st not have been tired with it. There came thither the finest Princess, the most beautiful ever was seen with mortal eyes. She showed us a thousand civilities and gave us oranges and citrons."

Cinderella seemed very indifferent in the matter. Indeed, she asked them the name of that Princess, but they told her they did not know it, and that the King's son was very uneasy on her account, and would give all the world to know who she was. At this Cinderella, smiling, replied:

"She must, then, be very beautiful indeed. How happy you have been! Could not I see her? Ah! dear Miss Charlotte, do lend me your yellow suit of clothes which you wear every day."

"Ay, to be sure," cried Miss Charlotte; "lend my clothes to such it dirty cinder maid as thou art! I should be a fool."

「ずいぶんとごゆっくりでしたのね」と大声を出し、あくびをして目をこすりながら、寝ていたところをちょうど起こされた、というように伸びをしました。でも、姉たちが外出してから、シンデレラは眠りたいなどとはこれっぽっちも思いませんでした。

「もしあんたも舞踏会に来てたらね」姉の1人が言いました、「絶対に飽きたりはしなかったわよ。最高のお姫様がいらしてね、だれも今まで見たこともないような、一番の美しさだったんだから。その方は私たちにとってもやさしくしてくださって、オレンジとミカンをくださったのよ」

シンデレラは、そのことにまったく関わりがないように見えました。実際のところ、彼女はそのお姫様の名前を姉たちに尋ねてみましたが、姉たちは名前を知らないと言いましたし、王様のご子息がお姫様のせいでとてもそわそわしていて、お姫様の正体を知るためなら、何でもするつもりだそうだ、と言っていました。これに、シンデレラは、微笑みながら答えました。

「それじゃ、その方は本当にお美しい方なんでしょうね。お幸せでしたわね、お姉様方。私もお目にかかりたかったわ。そうそう、シャーロットお嬢様。毎日お召しの黄色のおそろいの服を貸してくださいませんか」

「あっ、あのなあ」シャーロットお嬢様が大声を出しました、「アンタみてえな、こぎたねえ消し炭娘に、自分の服を貸すってか。そんなおバカじゃなくってよ」

シンデレラ (10) 63

as if	まるで〜のように	on her account	彼女のせいで
ask	尋ねる	out of	〜から
dear	〜さん	replied	< reply 返事をする
dirty	汚らしい	rub	こする
do	どうか、どうぞ	seem	〜のように見える
fool	愚か者、馬鹿者	since	〜以来、〜から
gape	あくびをする	sleep	寝ること、睡眠；寝る
give all the world to		smile	微笑む
〜のためならどんな犠牲も払う		stretch herself	伸びをする
happy	幸せな、幸運な	such	そのような、そんな
inclination to	〜したい気持ち	suit	そろい、スーツ
indeed	実に、実際のところ	tired with	〜に飽きて
indifferent in	〜に関係がない	to be sure	確かに
just	ちょうど	told	<tell 言う、話す
lend	貸す	uneasy	落ち着きがない
manner	種類	wake	目を覚まさせる、起こす
matter	こと	wear	着る、身に着ける
mortal	死ぬ運命にある、人の	yellow	黄色の
must	〜に違いない		

Cinderella expected well such answer and was very glad of the refusal, for she would have been sadly put to it if her sister had lent her what she asked for jestingly.

The next day the two sisters were at the ball, and so was Cinderella, but dressed more magnificently than before. The King's son was always by her, and never ceased his compliments and kind speeches to her, to whom all this was so far from being tiresome that she quite forgot what her Godmother had recommended to her, so that she at last counted the clock striking twelve when she took it to be no more than eleven. She then rose up and fled as nimble as a deer. The Prince followed, but could not overtake her. She left behind one of her glass slippers, which the Prince took up most carefully. She got home, but quite out of breath, and in her old clothes, having nothing left her of all her finery but one of the little slippers, fellow to that she dropped. The guards at the palace gate were asked if they had not seen a Princess go out.

They said they had seen nobody go out but a young girl, very meanly dressed, and who had more of the air of a poor country girl than a gentlewoman.

シンデレラは、そんな答えもあろうかと予想していましたし、断られてとてもうれしかったのです。だって、ふざけて頼んだものをお姉様が貸してくれたりしていたら、シンデレラは大変困った立場に追い込まれていたでしょうから。

翌日、2人の姉は舞踏会に出かけ、シンデレラも行きましたが、前日よりももっと立派に着飾っていました。王様のご子息はいつも彼女のそばにいて、決して褒め言葉を絶やしたり、彼女に親切な言葉を掛けるのをやめたりすることはありませんでした。シンデレラにとっても、こういったいろいろなことは退屈だなどということからはまったくほど遠く、教母様の言いつけを、すっかり忘れてしまっていました。そうしてついに、彼女は時計が12時を打つのを数えてしまいました。その時は彼女はまだ11時にすぎないと思っていたのですが。それから彼女は立ち上がり、シカのように軽快に逃げ出しました。王子様も追いかけましたが、シンデレラに追いつくことはできませんでした。彼女はガラスの靴の片方を置いてきてしまいました。そして王子は、それをとても大切に拾い上げました。シンデレラは家へたどり着きましたが、すっかり息が切れ、古びた衣服を身にまとい、豪華な衣装の数々のうち、残ったのは、かわいらしい靴の片方以外、すなわち彼女が落としてきたものの片割れ以外、何もありませんでした。宮殿の門番たちは、姫君が出て行くのを見かけなかったか、と尋ねられました。

門番は、みすぼらしい身なりの若い女性が出て行ったきりです、その人物は貴婦人というよりは田舎娘という感じでした、と答えました。

air	様子、雰囲気	go out	出る、外出する
answer	答え	got	<get home 帰宅する
ask if	～かと尋ねる、きく	guard	門番、守衛
ask for	求める、くれと頼む	jestingly	ふざけて、戯れに
at last	ついに、とうとう	kind	親切な、やさしい
be sadly put to it if	～だとひどく困る	left	<leave 残る
			leave behind 置き忘れる
breath	息	lent	<lend 貸す
but	～を除いて	magnificently	立派に、すばらしく
by	～の側に、傍らに	meanly	みすぼらしく
carefully	注意深く	most	とても
cease	やめる	nimble	軽快に、素早く
compliment	ほめ言葉	no more than	ほんの～にすぎない
count	数える	out of breath	息を切らして
country	田舎の	overtake	追いつく
deer	シカ	palace	宮殿、王宮
dressed	装っている	poor	みすぼらしい
drop	落とす	quite	とても、すっかり
expect	予想する、予期する	recommend	勧める、助言する
far from	～からはほど遠い	refusal	拒否、拒絶
fellow	片方、もう一方	rose	<rise up 立ち上がる
finery	豪華な衣装	slipper	（舞踏会用の）靴
fled	<flee 逃げる	speech	言葉
follow	追いかける	tiresome	退屈な
forgot	<forget 忘れる	took	<take
gate	門、城門	take ～ to	～を…と考える
gentlewoman	貴婦人	take up	拾い上げる

When the two sisters returned from the ball Cinderella asked them if they had been well diverted and if the beautiful Princess had been there.

They told her yes, but that she hurried away immediately when the clock struck twelve, and with so much haste that she dropped one of her little glass slippers, the prettiest in the world, which the King's son had taken up; that he had done nothing but look at her all the time at the ball, and that most certainly he was very much in love with the beautiful person who owned the glass slipper.

What they said was very true, for a few days after the King's son caused it to be proclaimed, by sound of trumpet, that he would marry her whose foot this slipper would just fit. They whom he employed began to try it upon the Princesses, then the Duchesses and all the Court, but in vain. It was brought to the two sisters, who did all they possibly could to thrust their feet into the slipper, but they could not effect it. On the following morning there was a great noise of trumpets and drums, and a procession passed through the town, at the head of which rode the King's son. Behind him came a herald, bearing a velvet cushion, upon which rested a little glass slipper. The herald blew a blast upon the trumpet, and then read a proclamation saying that the King's son would wed any lady in the land who could fit the slipper upon her foot, if she could produce another to match it.

　２人の姉が舞踏会から戻ると、シンデレラは姉たちに、十分に楽しめたか、例の美しいお姫様は来ていたか、と尋ねました。
　そうだが、時計が１２時を打つと、お姫様はすぐに急いでどこかへ行ってしまい、とても急いだのでガラスの靴の片方を落としていってしまった。それは世界中で最もかわいらしいもので、それを王子が拾い上げた。王子は舞踏会のあいだ中ずっと、お姫様のことを見つめるだけだったし、きっと間違いなく王子様はガラスの靴の持ち主に、深く恋しているに違いない、と姉たちはシンデレラに話しました。
　姉たちが言ったことはまったく真実でした。なぜなら数日後、王様のご息子はトランペットの音とともに、王子はこの靴がぴったり合う足の人と結婚する、と布告させたのでした。王子の雇い人たちが、王女たちに試しに履かせ始め、次に公妃たちに、それから宮廷の者たちみなに。でも無駄でした。２人の姉妹のもとにも靴がもたらされ、靴の中に足を押し込もうと、できることは何でもしてみましたが、履くことはできませんでした。翌朝、トランペットと太鼓の音が大音響で鳴り響き、街を行列が通り、その先頭を王様のご息子が馬に乗って進んで行きました。その後ろにはお触れ役が、ビロードのクッションを携え、その上には小さなガラスの靴が載っていました。お触れ役はトランペットをひと吹きすると、次に布告を読み上げました。国王の息子は、国内で例の靴が足の大きさと合う女性と結婚する、もしその女性がもう片方の靴を差し出すことができれば、という内容のものでした。

シンデレラ (12)

a few days after	数日後	in vain	無駄で、役に立たない
all the time	いつも、始終	land	国、国土
another	もう1つ別の	little	小さな、かわいらしい
any	どんな	look at	～を見る
at the head of	～の先頭に	marry	～と結婚する
bear	持つ、捧げ持つ	match	合う、対になる
behind	～の後ろに、次に	noise	大きな音、物音
blast	ひと吹き	own	持つ、所有する
blew	<blow 吹く	pass through	～を通り過ぎる
brought	<bring	person	ひと、人物
cause	～させる	possibly	できるかぎり
certainly	確かに、確実に	prettiest	<pretty
court	宮廷	procession	行列
cushion	クッション、当て布	proclaim	宣言する、布告する
diverted	気が晴れて、楽しんで	proclamation	宣言、布告
do nothing but	～しかしない	produce	取り出す、出して見せる
drum	太鼓	rest	載っている
duchess	公妃	return	もどる
effect	成功させる、達成する	rode	<ride 馬に乗って行く
employ	用いる、雇う	sound	音
feet	<foot 足	thrust	ぐいっと押し込む
fit	合う、合わせる	thrust into	～に押し込める
following	次の	town	街
glass	ガラスの、ガラス製の	true	正しい、真実の
haste	あわてること、いそぎ	trumpet	トランペット、ラッパ
head	先頭	try	試しに身に着けさせる
herald	お触れ役	velvet	ビロードの
hurry away	急いで去る	wed	結婚する
in love with	～に恋して		

Of course, the sisters tried to squeeze their feet into the slipper, but it was of no use--they were much too large. Then Cinderella shyly begged that she might try. How the sisters laughed with scorn when the Prince knelt to fit the slipper on the cinder maid's foot; but what was their surprise when it slipped on with the greatest ease, and the next moment Cinderella produced the other from her pocket! Once more she stood in the slippers, and once more the sisters saw before them the lovely Princess who was to be the Prince's bride. For at the touch of the magic shoes the little gray frock disappeared forever, and in place of it she wore the beautiful robe the fairy Godmother had given to her.

The sisters hung their heads with sorrow and vexation; but kind little Cinderella put her arms round their necks, kissed them, and forgave them for all their unkindness, so that they could not help but love her.

The Prince could not bear to part from his little love again, so he carried her back to the palace in his grand coach, and they were married that very day. Cinderella's stepsisters were present at the feast, but in the place of honor sat the fairy Godmother.

So the poor little cinder maid married the Prince, and in time they came to be King and Queen, and lived happily ever after.

　もちろん、姉妹は靴に足を押し込もうとしましたが、無駄でした。足が大き過ぎたのです。するとシンデレラが恥ずかしがりながら、やらせてもらえないか、と願い出ました。姉妹は、消し炭娘の足下に王子が靴を合わせるためにひざまずくと、あざけり笑いました。ですが、ふたりの驚きはなんとしたことだったでしょう。靴はとても楽々と足にはまり、次の瞬間にはシンデレラが、ポケットからもう片方の靴を出すではありませんか。再びシンデレラが、その靴を両方履いて立ち上がると、再び姉妹は目の前に、王子様の花嫁となるべきすてきなお姫様を見たのでした。なぜかというと、魔法の靴に触れた瞬間に、きつめのねずみ色の作業着は永遠に消えてなくなり、その代わりに、シンデレラは教母様がくださった美しい衣装を身にまとっていたのでした。

　姉妹は失望し、腹立たしくて、首をうなだれました。でも、やさしいシンデレラちゃんは、姉さんたちの肩に両腕を回し、キスしました。そうして姉さんたちの、ありとあらゆる意地悪を許してあげました。今や姉さんたちも、シンデレラを愛さないわけにはいきません。

arms	両腕	neck	首、肩
at the touch of	～が触れた瞬間	of no use	役に立たない、ダメな
bear	耐える、我慢する	of course	もちろん
before	～の前に	once more	もう一度、再び
beg	乞い願う、懇願する	other	別の、他の
bride	花嫁	part	別れる
carry	（乗せて）運ぶ	pocket	ポケット
could not help but	～せずにはいられなかった	present	出席して
disappear	消える、消えてなくなる	produce	取り出す
ever after	それからずっと	queen	王妃、妃
feast	宴、祝いの席、祝宴	robe	優雅な服、礼服、式服
forever	永遠に	round	～の回りに
forgave	<forgive 許す	scorn	軽蔑、あざけり
frock	作業着、仕事着	shoes	靴
grand	壮大な、立派な	shyly	はずかしげに、控えめに
head	首	slip on	すっと入る
honor	名誉	sorrow	悲しみ、残念、無念
in the place of honor	名誉ある場所、上座、上席	squeeze into	～へ押し込める
		stepsister	まま姉妹
hung	<hang うなだれる	stood	<stand 立つ、立ち上がる
in place of	～の代わりに	surprise	驚き
in time	やがて	too	～すぎる
kind	やさしい、親切な	touch	触れること、接触
kiss	キスする	try	試みる
knelt	<kneel ひざまずく	unkindness	不親切
lived happily	幸せに暮らしました	very	まさにその
love	愛する；愛しい人	vexation	いらだたせること
magic	魔法の	with ease	やさしく、簡単に
much	ずっと	wore	<wear 着る、身に着ける

　王子様は、このかわいらしい人ともう二度と別れることに我慢がならず、シンデレラを自分の立派な馬車に乗せて宮殿へと連れ帰り、2人はまさにその日のうちに結婚しました。シンデレラのまま姉妹も宴に出席しましたが、一番の席に座ったのは妖精の教母様でした。

　このように、かわいそうな消し炭お嬢ちゃんは、王子様と結婚し、やがて2人は王と王妃となり、ずっと幸せに暮らしました。

練習問題

The Dog and the Shadow

Questions

Write T(rue) if the sentence is correct, or write F(alse) if the answer is wrong.

1 _   The dog was swimming across a river.

2 _   The dog found peace in the water.

3 _   The meat that the other dog had looked more delicious.

4 _   The dog lost all the meat.

****

肉をくわえた犬のイラストを描いてみましょう。

練習問題 73

Let's try!
日本語にしてみましょう

Not the children of the rich or of the powerful only, but of all alike, boys and girls, both noble and ignoble, rich and poor, in all cities and towns, villages and hamlets, should be sent to school.

John Amos Comenius　（コメニウス）
The Great Didactic, 1649
Translated by M.W. Keatinge, 1896

(日本語訳)

_____

_____

_____

_____

(感想・コメント)

_____

_____

not ... only, but ~ alike ...だけでなく、〜も		children < child 子ども
the rich　金持ち	the powerful　権力者	only　〜だけ
alike　同じく、同様に	noble　貴族の	ignoble　生まれの卑しい
rich　金持ちの	poor　貧しい	cities < city　都市、都会
town　町	village　村	hamlet　集落、村落
should　〜すべきである	be sent　送られる	

The Wolf in Sheep's Clothing

Questions

1 What did the Wolf decide to do in order to prey upon a flock of sheep?

　_____

　_____

2 Could the wolf deceive the Shepherd?

　_____

　_____

3 Who killed the wolf?

　_____

　_____

How?

　_____

　_____

Why?

　_____

　_____

練習問題 75

リンカーンの言葉より

−立場変われば−

The shepherd drives the wolf from the sheep's throat, for which the sheep thanks the shepherd as his liberator, while the wolf denounces him for the same act as the destroyer of liberty.

Abraham Lincoln (1809-1865)

日本語にしてみましょう。

_____

_____

_____

_____

_____

_____

drive 追い払う　throat のど　　liberator 解放者(liberate 解放する、自由にする)
while 〜の間、〜の一方　　　denounce 公然と非難する　　　act 行為
destroyer 破壊者 (destroy 破壊する)　　liberty 自由

The Farmer and His Sons

Questions

1 What did the Farmer do when he was going to die?

_____

_____

2 What did the father say to his sons?

_____

_____

3 What did the sons do when their father died?

_____

_____

4 Did the sons find what they wanted?

_____

5 What did the sons of the Farmer learn from their father?

_____

_____

The Child is Father of the Man?

日本語にしてみましょう

Human beings are the only creatures that allow their children to come back home.

_____

_____

Antoine de Saint-Exupery (1900-1944)

The first half of our lives is ruined by our parents, and the second half by our children.

_____

_____

Clarence Darrow (1857-1938)

If your parents never had children, chances are you won't, either.
　　　　[あなたの親に子どもがいなければ、あなたは存在しないはず、ですね]

_____

_____

Dick Cavett(1936-)

英語のことわざ
　　Boys will be boys.

_____

　　Like father, like son.

_____

human beings 人間　　　　creature 生き物　　　　allow 許す
ruin 壊す、だいなしにする　　chances are 〜の可能性は高い

The Hare and the Tortoise

Questions

1 The Tortoise thought he would never win the race.
    True / False

2 The Fox was the time keeper.   T / F

3 While the Hare was fast asleep, the Tortoise also had a good rest.   T / F

4 At the race, the Tortoise started first, because the fox wanted to talk with the Hare.   T / F

5 Do you have anything that you keep on doing, for example, playing the piano, jogging, studying English? What is it? Tell me.

_____

_____

_____

_____

練習問題 79

違いは何でしょう。

　　turtle　　　_____

　　tortoise　 _____

　　rabbit　　 _____

　　hare　　　 _____

　　bunny　　 _____

これって何？

　　bunny girl　_____

（興味ある方は自己責任で次のアドレスのページを。もちろん英語です。

http://www.playboy.com/casinos-gaming/pbcasinos/080299/3.html）

　　rabbit hutch　_____

　　Peter Rabbit　_____

　　Bugs Bunny　_____

ことわざコーナー

First catch your hare then cook him.

_____

****

We have been God-like in our planned breeding of our domesticated plants and animals, but we have been rabbit-like in our unplanned breeding of ourselves.

　　　　　　　　　　　　Arnold Toynbee (1889-1975)

The Fox and the Crow

次は、キツネとカラスの話を書き直したものです。下線部に、与えられた語から適切なものを入れなさい（複数回使用可）。

A ____ was sitting on a branch of a tree with a piece of ____ in her mouth. Then a ____ looked at her very carefully to find a way to get the cheese in his ____ .

When the fox ____ to the tree, he ____ under the tree and ____ up, then he said, "What a great bird I see above me! She is the most beautiful bird I have ever seen. The color of her body is so ____ . She is really beautiful. If her voice is as beautiful as her ____ , she must be the queen of the birds, I am sure."

The ____ was very happy to hear that, and she wanted to ____ that she could sing very well. Then she sang very loudly. Of course, the cheese went down from her mouth, and the ____ took it. Finally, the ____ said, "Lady, you can sing, I understand that. But you are not very clever."

came	cheese	crow	fox
hands	looked	looks	lovely
show	stood		

練習問題 81

ルソーの『エミール』(英語訳)の一節です。省略されている部分に注意して、日本語にしてみましょう。

We are born weak, we need strength; helpless, we need aid; foolish, we need reason. All that we lack at birth, all that we need when we come to man's estate, is the gift of education.

Jean-Jacques Rousseau, Emile

****

weak 弱い　　strength 強さ、力　　helpless 無力な　　aid 助け
foolish おろかな　　reason 理性　　lack 欠ける、不足する
at birth 生まれた時、誕生時　　come to man's estate 成人する
gift 賜物、与えてくれるもの　　education 教育

The Fox and the Stork

Questions

Circle T if it is true, or circle F if it is false.

1 T / F   First, a fox invited a stork for breakfast.

2 T / F   The fox provided a variety of food on a large flat dish.

3 T / F   The stork did not enjoy eating the food at the fox's place, because she didn't like it.

4 T / F   The happy face of the stork made the fox also happy.

5 T / F   The stork invited the fox for dinner in turn, because the stork enjoyed the fox's company.

6 T / F   At the stork's house, they played baseball.

7 T / F   At the stork's place, the fox ate a lot because he was hungry.

読みましょう

マタイによる福音書 5.38-42

You have heard that it was said, 'Eye for eye, and tooth for tooth.'	モーセの法律では、『人の目をえぐり出した者は、自分の目もえぐり出される。人の歯を折った者は、自分の歯も折られる』とあります。
But I tell you, Do not resist an evil person. If someone strikes you on the right cheek, turn to him the other also.	しかし、わたしはあえて言いましょう。暴力に暴力で手向かってはいけません。もし右の頬をなぐられたら、左の頬も向けてやりなさい。
And if someone wants to sue you and take your tunic, let him have your cloak as well.	借金のかたに下着を取り上げようとする人には、上着もやりなさい。
If someone forces you to go one mile, go with him two miles.	荷物を1キロ先まで運べと命令されたら、2キロ先まで運んでやりなさい。
Give to the one who asks you, and do not turn away from the one who wants to borrow from you.	何かくださいと頼む人には与え、借りに来た人を手ぶらで追い返さないようにしなさい。
From <u>New International Version</u>	『リビングバイブル』より

* * * * * * * * * * * * *

You have heard it was said 言われたこと（つまり、モーセが言ったこと）を聞いている　resist 抵抗する　　　evil 悪い　　　strike 打つ、たたく　　cheek 頬
the other = the other cheek　　sue 訴える
tunic チェニカ（古代ローマ人が着た2枚の布を肩口と両脇のところで縫い合わせた服）　cloak マント　　as well 〜も　　　force 強いる、強制する
turn away そっぽを向く　　borrow （金を）借りる

The Northwind and the Sun

Questions

話の順に並べ替えなさい。

1. Each insisted that he was the stronger of the two.
2. Then, the Sun gently shone upon the tourist and proved that he is the wiser.
3. The North Wind and the Sun had a quarrel.
4. First, the North Wind tried in vain.
5. So, they decided to try their powers on a tourist.

____ → ____ → ____ → ____ → ____

意味の似ている語句を右から選びなさい

claim	_____
dispute	_____
at last	_____
agree	_____
force	_____
cloak	_____
wrap	_____

be of the same opinion
coat
cover
finally
insist
power
quarrel

練習問題 85

西から昇ったお日様が〜

カッコには漢字を、下線部には英語を入れましょう。

　日本語で方角をいう時の順番は、（　）（　）（　）（　）
ですが、英語では、_____ _____ _____ _____
という順になります。中国語では、（　）（　）（　）（　）
ですね。このように、文化によってものごとの言い表し方が異なる場合
があります。

****

それぞれ単語を入れましょう

　　方角　　　　　　　〜の
　　north　　　　　　 northern
　　south　　　　　　 _____
　　east　　　　　　　_____
　　west　　　　　　　_____

（吹き出し）プロ野球２軍チームのリーグ名にもなってます。そうそう、映画のジャンルにもありましたネ　フルイ？

映画、小説のタイトル。長編です。
　　Gone with the _____　　『風と共に去りぬ』
「日本」は、日出づる国、ともいわれます　the _____ Sun

ヘミングウェーの小説です。映画化もされていますね。
　　The Sun Also _____ は『日はまた昇る』です。
　　Farewell to Arms と言えば、『手を振ってバイバイ』ではなく、
　　_____

もう一問。サザンオールスターズはSouthern All Starsのようですが、
サウザン（あるいはサザン）アイランドと呼ばれるプチプチがいっぱい
入っているサラダドレッシングは英語で？　_____

The Goose that Laid the Golden Eggs

Answer in English.

1 What kind of goose did the man and his wife get?

2 What did the man and wife begin to think?

3 What did they decide to do?

4 What did they find in the body of the goose?

5 What did you learn from this story? Explain.

Is This a Piece of Cake?

おもしろい英語の表現を、2つ覚えておきましょう。

You can't have your cake and eat it (too).

_____

もう1つは、見出しになっている、
It's a piece of cake.
　　　こちらは、チョウ _____ 。

****

ついでに、ガチョウに関係するものも2つ。

All his geese are swans.

_____

The old woman is picking her goose.

_____

****

ガチョウのおまけ
goose pimples / goose flesh _____

goose eggはガチョウの卵ですが、試験で取ってしまうとイヤーなものナーンダ？　_____

Three Little Pigs (1)

Questions

Circle T or F : T for true, F for false.

1   T / F

   The mother pig was very rich and wanted to let her sons see the outside world and let them have real experience of the real world.

2   T / F

   The first pig made his house with plastics.

3   T / F

   The wolf broke down the house of the first little pig.

4   T / F

   The first little pig and the wolf were good friends.

5   T / F

   The wolf ate up the first little pig.

****

動物とお肉との関係はいかに？

	動物	食用
ブタ	pig	
ウシ		beef
ヒツジ	sheep	

ブタさんの代表的な呼び方を覚えておきましょう。

　　　　　　メスブタ　　　　＿＿＿＿＿＿＿

　　　　　　オスブタ　　　　＿＿＿＿＿＿＿

　　　　　　子ブタ　　　　　＿＿＿＿＿＿＿

＜クイズ＞

第1問　トンカツは好きですか？
　　　トンカツの「トン」は「豚」ですね。
　　　では「カツ」はなんでしょう。　　　＿＿＿＿＿＿＿

第2問　fortune-teller は何をする人？
　　　　　　　　　　　　　　　　　　　　＿＿＿＿＿＿＿

第3問　Let me come in. の let は「〜させる」という意味ですネ。
　　　テニスをするとき、サーブがネットに触れて、ちゃんとコートに入ると、審判が「レット」とコールします。ウインブルドン大会の中継などでもおなじみの光景で、そのあと、低い声で、「ファーストサービス」などと言っています。さて、この「レット」は何でしょう。
　　　　　　　　　　　　　　　　　　　　＿＿＿＿＿＿＿

第4問　アルファベットで書いてみましょう。

　　　　　お化粧に使うのは　　　　パフ　　　＿＿＿＿＿＿＿

　　　　　Aml Yumlで　　　　　　パフィ　　＿＿＿＿＿＿＿

　　　　　デザートは　　　　　　　パフェ　　＿＿＿＿＿＿＿

Three Little Pigs (2)

Questions

さて、子豚たちの運命はどうなったでしょう。まとめておきましょう。

	house material	dead or alive
1st pig		
2nd pig		
3rd pig		

再確認です。単語を入れて完成させましょう。

The first little pig built a house with _____, but a wolf came and _____ the house in. So the poor little pig was _____ by the wolf.

The second little pig built a house with _____. Again, the wolf came and blew the house _____. And the wolf _____ the poor second little pig.

The third little pig built his house with _____. Yet again, the wolf came and tried to blow the house in. But the house was

_____.

_____.
（「じょうぶだったので．．．」と英語で書いてみましょう）

オトコハ　オオカミ　ナノヨ

かどうかは、知りませんが、オオカミと豚に関する英語をみてみましょう。

　　　a man in sheep's clothingの意味は、以前に読んだお話から想像がつきますね。　　_____

cry wolf　_____（意味）
　　　これをするのは、オオカミ少年、いえいえ本当は羊飼いの少年ですね。オオカミがきたぞー！と叫んでばかりいて、しまいには誰にも信じてもらえなくなった少年です。ちなみに、オオカミに育てられた（とおぼしき）子どもはa wolf child といいます。

満月の夜、変身するのはオオカミ男。英語では　_____　。
　　　　　　（ハリー・ポッターのルピン先生、これでしたね。）

次の２つは（日本語では）豚に関係する英語の表現です。対応する日本語のことわざはなんでしょう。

　　　casting pearls before swine

_____

　　　Flattery will work wonders.　[flattery お世辞、ごますり]

_____

最後に英作文。考えてみましょう。「男はオオカミなのよ」

_____

Three Little Pigs (3)

Questions

Circle T or F : T for true, F for false.

1   T / F

    The wolf huffed and puffed very hard, and finally he could blow the brick house down.

2   T / F

    The wolf knew where there was a nice field of tulips.

3   T / F

    The next morning, the little pig got up at 5.

4   T / F

    The little pig called on the wolf as the pig promised.

5   T / F

    The wolf came to the house of the little pig at 6.

6   T / F

    The wolf and the little pig went out together to Mr. Smith's field.

7   T / F

    The wolf was very angry when he found that the little pig had been and come back with a nice potful for dinner.

練習問題 93

1 ディズニーのアニメ映画、『三匹の子豚』が作られたのはいつのことでしょう。調べてみましょう

_____年。

2 主題歌、「オオカミなんかこわくない」は英語では

W____'s Afraid of the B____   B____   Wolf.

ついでに英語版の歌詞の始まりのところを書き留めておきましょう

_____

_____

_____

_____

3 次に、fieldという単語の勉強です。意味を書き込みましょう。

rice field _____   football field _____

oil field _____   battlefield _____

air field _____   track and field _____

field day _____   field work _____

4 最後に、カブはturnipでしたが、株式会社の「株」は英語で一般的には _____ 。東京証券取引所は、英語で

Tokyo _____ _____

Three Little Pigs (4)

Questions

1. What time did the little pig get up to get the nice apples and why?

2. Was the little pig happy on the tree when he saw the wolf coming? How did he feel?

3. What did the little pig do when the wolf came to him?

4. What was going on at Shanklin that afternoon?

赤いリンゴに…

1 エデンの園でアダムが食べたと言われている木の実は

　　　　　　　　　　　　　　　　　　　　　　　_____

2 果物といえばリンゴ。ことわざもたくさんあります。

　　An apple a day keeps the doctor away.
　　_____

　　The apples on the other side of the wall are the sweetest.
　　_____

　　The rotten apple injures its neighbor.
　　_____
　　　　　　　　　　　　　　　　（金八先生ではみかん？）

3 リンゴの品種をあげてみましょう。いくついえるかな？

　　_____　　_____　　_____

　　_____　　_____　　_____

4 the Big Apple と呼ばれる都市はどこでしょう。

　　　　　　　　　　　　　　　　　　　　　_____

Three Little Pigs (5)

Questions

次の質問を英語で作成し、英語で答えなさい。

1　子豚はオオカミと市へ行きましたか。

　　　Q _____
　　　A _____

2　子豚は市で何を買いましたか。

　　　Q _____
　　　A _____
　　　　_____

3　なぜ子豚はかく乳機の中に隠れたのですか。

　　　Q _____
　　　A _____

4　最後にはオオカミはどうなりましたか。

　　　Q _____
　　　A _____
　　　　_____

マイ・フェア…

1　フェア・レディーという車がありますね。英語で書くとどうなるのでしょうか。

　　　　　　　　　　　　　　　＿＿＿＿＿＿＿＿

2　野球です。バッター、打ちました。フェアーかファールか？

　　　　　　　　フェアー　　＿＿＿＿＿＿＿＿

　　　　　　　　ファール　　＿＿＿＿＿＿＿＿

　ついでに、フェアプレー賞、なんていうのもあります。

　　　　　　　　　　　　　　　＿＿＿＿＿＿＿＿

　　おまけ：ブックフェアは：　＿＿＿＿＿＿＿＿

3　ご存知、『メアリー・ポピンズ』にはちょっと聞くと、「チンチムニー」と始まる歌があります。どんな歌なのでしょうか。歌詞を調べてみましょう。

　　＿＿＿＿＿＿＿＿＿＿＿＿＿＿＿＿＿＿＿＿＿＿＿＿
　　＿＿＿＿＿＿＿＿＿＿＿＿＿＿＿＿＿＿＿＿＿＿＿＿
　　＿＿＿＿＿＿＿＿＿＿＿＿＿＿＿＿＿＿＿＿＿＿＿＿
　　＿＿＿＿＿＿＿＿＿＿＿＿＿＿＿＿＿＿＿＿＿＿＿＿
　　＿＿＿＿＿＿＿＿＿＿＿＿＿＿＿＿＿＿＿＿＿＿＿＿

The Bremen Town-Musicians (1)

Questions

テキストからそのまま抜き出さないで、自分で考えて書いてみましょう。

1 Why did the donkey run away from his master?

_____

_____

_____

2 What did the donkey find when he had walked some distance?

   Animal: _____

   What did the animal say?

   _____

   _____

   _____

   _____

The Bremen Town-Musicians (2)

Questions

テキストからそのまま抜き出さないで、自分の考えを答えましょう。

1 What were the donkey and the hound going to play?

2 The cat was in danger of his life. Why was he?

The Bremen Town-Musicians (3)

Questions

1   What was the matter with the crow?

2   What was the donkey's advice?

The Bremen Town-Musicians (4)

Questions

1. Where were they going to sleep in the forest?

	donkey	hound	cat	cock
place				

2. Who found the robber's house?

   _____

3. Who looked into the window of the robber's house?

   _____

The Bremen Town-Musicians (5)

Questions

1   What did the donkey find?

_____

_____

2   In their plan, how were they going to place themselves?

4		
3		
2		
1		
	animal	place/position

The Bremen Town-Musicians (6)

Questions

1. How did they perform their music?

    The donkey _____ .
    The hound   _____ .
    The cat   _____ .
    The cock   _____ .

2. What did the robbers think when they heard the music? And what did they do?

    _____

    _____

3. What did the four musicians did then?

    _____

    _____

4. Where did they sleep?

	donkey	hound	cat	cock
place				

The Bremen Town-Musicians (7)

Questions

1 What did the messenger do first when he came back to the house?

   _____

   _____

2 What did the animals do then?

   (1) The cat _____

   _____

   (2) Next the dog _____

   _____

   (3) And the donkey _____

   _____

   (4) Also the cock _____

   _____

The Bremen Town-Musicians (8)

Questions

1   The messenger reported to the captain that he saw:

place	what	action
in the house		
by the door		
in the yard		
upon the roof		

2   What did the four musicians do then?

_____

_____

■編訳者紹介

内桶　真二（うちおけ　しんじ）

1962年生まれ
1993年　　青山学院大学大学院文学研究科英語英文学専攻博士
　　　　　後期課程単位取得済退学
現　在　　茨城女子短期大学国文科講師
　　　　　青山学院大学非常勤講師
専門分野　英語学・英語史

英語で楽しむ昔話

2006年4月30日　初版第1刷発行

■編　訳　者——内桶　真二
■発　行　者——佐藤　守
■発　行　所——株式会社 大学教育出版
　　　　　　　〒700-0953　岡山市西市855-4
　　　　　　　電話(086)244-1268㈹　FAX(086)246-0294
■印刷製本——サンコー印刷㈱
■装　　　丁——原　美穂

Ⓒ Shinji UCHIOKE 2006, Printed in Japan
検印省略　落丁・乱丁本はお取り替えいたします。
無断で本書の一部または全部を複写・複製することは禁じられています。

ISBN4-88730-694-6